CAREERS IN COUNSELING
AND
HUMAN SERVICES

CAREERS IN COUNSELING AND HUMAN SERVICES
Second Edition

Edited by

Brooke B. Collison
Associate Professor and Coordinator
Counselor Education
Oregon State University
Corvallis, Oregon

Nancy J. Garfield
Supervisor of Counseling Psychology
Director of Training
Colmery-O'Neil VA Medical Center
Topeka, Kansas

Taylor & Francis
Publishers since 1798

USA	Publishing Office:	Taylor & Francis
		1101 Vermont Ave., NW,
		Suite 200
		Washington, DC 20005
		Tel: (202) 289-2174
		Fax: (202) 289-3665
	Distribution Center:	Taylor & Francis
		1900 Frost Road, Suite 101
		Bristol, PA 19007-1598
		Tel: (215) 785-5800
		Fax: (215) 785-5515
UK		Taylor & Francis, Ltd.
		4 John Street
		London WC1N 2ET
		Tel: 071 405 2237
		Fax: 071 831 2035

CAREERS IN COUNSELING AND HUMAN SERVICES, Second Edition

2 3 4 5 6 7 8 9 0 BRBR 0 9 8 7 6

This book was set in Times Roman. Technical development and editing by Bernadette Capelle. Cover design by Michelle Fleitz. Printing and binding by Braun-Brumfield, Inc.

A CIP catalog record for this book is available from the British Library.
(∞) The paper in this publication meets the requirements of the ANSI Standard Z39.48-1984 (Permanence of Paper)

Library of Congress Cataloging-in-Publication Data
Careers in counseling and human services/edited by Brooke B. Collison, Nancy J. Garfield.—2nd ed.
    p. cm.
Rev. ed. of: Careers in counseling and human development. c1994.
Includes biographical references and index.

    1. Counseling—Vocational guidance. I. Collison, Brooke B. II. Garfield, Nancy J. III. Careers in counseling and human development.
BF637.C6C325 1995
361.3'23'02373—dc20   95-41278
                                                                        CIP
ISBN 1-56032-415-5

R
650.1402436l
C271c2

Dedication

We dedicate this book to our good friend and colleague--Rosalie Deckert, MD. Rose was the kind of helping professional we both admire. A practicing physician, she was a counselor and true helping professional in her practice of medicine. Her work was made more difficult in the past several years because of her battle with cancer. That didn't slowed her down--she continued to practice in that broad-based human service approach that seems to be missing from many of the professionals we see. We hope that this book will encourage more people like Rose to enter the counseling and human services professions, and that it will demonstrate to her son, Sundance, and husband, Joe, the professional and interpersonal impact she had during her life.

NJG & BBC

Contents

Contents

Preface

This book is a revision of *Careers in Counseling and Human Development*. The new title, *Careers in Counseling and Human Services* represents changes that we believe are significant: there is a continuing shift in this country to broaden the range and delivery methods of all the health and human services. Earlier, it was possible to discuss "counseling" as a singular subject--no longer. People considering a "helping profession" will find that the array of opportunities continues to expand. Similarly, preparation, licensure, delivery, compensation, and other aspects are changing. The chapter authors in this book call attention to some of those changes while saying that it is difficult to project other changes that will take place in the next few years.

The first edition of this book was used in many different settings. We received reports from students who used the first edition to assist in making career choices, from teachers who used the book in undergraduate classes, and from persons who had placed it in the career resource section of their libraries. We were delighted to hear that the first edition was, "one of the most frequently stolen books in the career resource room."

We were concerned that information in the first edition was dated; thus, the revision was needed. We found that more than half of the professional associations, licensing agencies, and accreditation boards listed in the first edition had either changed their name or address since 1990--a disturbing thought for us, since a common suggestion in the book is to tell readers to, "Contact the professional association listed in the Appendix." We hope that the current list is accurate for a few years.

We thank the chapter authors who wrote to our outlines and Elaine Pirrone and Bernadette Capelle with Taylor and Francis who have been gently persuasive in keeping us on task. We have enjoyed working together on this project--even though we had to do it by long distance. Thank goodness for electronic mail and fax machines.

BBC & NJG

Contributors

JEANNIE BEAMAN, MSW, ACSW, a licensed Specialist in Clinical Social Work, is a staff social worker at the Colmery-O'Neil Veterans Affairs Medical Center in Topeka, Kansas. She also has a private practice. Jeannie is a member of the National Association of Social Work and holds accreditation as an ACSW. She was formerly the Coordinator of the Social Work Student Training Program at Colmery-O'Neil VAMC, and provides supervision for social workers seeking the Clinical Social Work license.

BURT BERTRAM, Ed.D., LMFT, LMHC, has been in private practice since 1977. He is a partner in *Inner Change Facilitators, Inc.*, a consulting, training, and counseling firm in Orlando, Florida. He is also an Adjunct Professor of Counseling at Rollins College in Winter Park, Florida.

BROOKE B. COLLISON, Ph.D., NCC, LPC, is an Associate Professor and Coordinator of Counselor Education at Oregon State University. He is a former president of the American Counseling Association.

BETH DURODOYE, Ed.D., is an Assistant Professor of Counselor Education at the University of North Texas, where she specializes in the area of cross-cultural counseling. Dr. Durodoye serves on the Ethics Committee of the American Counseling Association.

DENNIS W. ENGELS, Ph.D., is Regents Professor of Counselor Education at the University of North Texas, Denton. His research and scholarly interests center on career development, decision making, ethics, human resource development, multipotentiality, and organizational and disciplinary history. He is President of the National Career Development Association. Dennis has consulted with public and private sector organizations and agencies throughout the United States.

NANCY J. GARFIELD, Ph.D., is a licensed psychologist in Kansas, Supervisor of Counseling Psychology and Director of Training at Colmery-O'Neil VA Medical Center, Topeka, Kansas. She frequently participates as a site evaluator for accreditation visits for the American Psychological Association and is a former member of the Kansas Board of Psychological Examiners.

LINDA K. GAST, Ph.D., is Director of the Career Center and an Affiliate Assistant Professor in Counseling and Personnel Services at the University of Maryland-College Park. She served as the first Editor of the ACPA Career Center Directors' National Data Bank, was elected to the executive boards of the Midwest Association of Colleges and Employers and the Middle Atlantic Association of Colleges and Employers, and has been an active member of the National Association of Colleges and Employers, the National Association of Student Personnel Administrators, and the American College Personnel Association.

BREE HAYES, Ed.D. is a consultant with RHR International Company in Atlanta, Georgia. She was formerly on the faculty of the University of Georgia. Bree is a past president of the Association for Specialists in Group Work and is Vice President of the Association for Humanistic Education and Development. She also serves on the Board of Directors for the National Board for Certified Counselors.

ANDREW A. HELWIG, Ph.D. is a Professor in Counseling and Personnel Services in the School of Education at the University of Colorado at Denver. He has worked as an employment counselor and was a state supervisor with the Job Service in Wisconsin. He is an NCC and NCCC. Andy is a past president of the National Employment Counselors Association.

CAROLYN KERN, Ph.D., NCC, LPC, is an Assistant Professor in Counseling and Student Services Administration at the University of North Texas in Denton, Texas. Previously she was a university counseling center clinical counselor and career counselor, as well as a residence hall director at Oklahoma State University. She is a member of the American Counseling Association, American Association for Counselor Education and Supervision, American School Counselor Association, American College Personnel Association, and American Educational Research Association.

SUSAN R. KOMIVES, Ph.D., is an Associate Professor in Counseling and Personnel Services and Faculty Associate in the Division of Student Affairs at the University of Maryland, College Park. Previously she was Vice President for Student Development at the University of Tampa and Stephens College, and has held other student affairs positions at Denison University and the University of Tennessee Knoxville. She is a Past President of the American College Personnel Association

RUTH TORKELSON LYNCH, Ph.D. is an Assistant Professor in the Department of Rehabilitation Psychology and Special Education at the University of Wisconsin-Madison. She previously held positions as staff rehabilitation counselor and as director of vocational services for the University of Wisconsin Hospital and Clinics Rehabilitation Center. Dr. Lynch is a former board member of the American Rehabilitation Counseling Association. She received her Ph.D. in rehabilitation counseling psychology from the University of Wisconsin-Madison.

ROSS K. LYNCH, Ph.D. is a rehabilitation psychologist and president of Professional Rehabilitation Services, Ltd., a multi disciplinary rehabilitation clinic located in Madison, Wisconsin. Dr. Lynch is a past president of the American Rehabilitation Counseling Association. He received his Ph.D. in rehabilitation counseling psychology from the University of Wisconsin-Madison.

PAMELA O. PAISLEY, Ed.D. is an Assistant Professor in the Department of Counseling and Human Development Services at the University of Georgia in Athens, Georgia, where she coordinates the school counseling program. She is President of the Southern Association for Counselor Education and Supervision. Pam recently co-authored a book on developmental school counseling programs.

CLAIRE COLE VAUGHT, Ed.D. is Associate Professor of Counselor Education at Virginia Tech in Blacksburg, VA. A former high school and middle school counselor, she has written several books and monographs on school counseling, as well as numerous articles. She is a former editor of *The School Counselor* and past president of the Virginia Counselors Association. Her particular interests are middle school counseling, teacher-advisor programs, and leadership development.

Chapter 1

AN INTRODUCTION TO THE PROFESSION

Brooke B. Collison
Nancy J. Garfield

Many people would like to have a career in which they help others, but they may not know about the various occupations in the counseling and human services fields, nor do they understand the differences and similarities among those occupations. This book provides information about careers in the counseling and human services fields. Most people know the school guidance counselor who assisted in choosing classes for the next school year, or administered an interest inventory for information about possible career choices. In this book, we provide information about school counselors and many other helping professionals who work with clients to help them solve problems.

This book provides general information about the fields of counseling and human services as well as the qualities of people who enter those fields: What are those people like and who are they? We will also discuss the types of educational programs you must attend to become a helping professional. The first two chapters include a discussion of changes that are taking place in the helping professions and suggest to readers that there are social, economic, and political forces that have an impact on careers in the helping professions.

No two jobs are ever alike, even if they have the same occupational title. You may find that the description of an occupation in one chapter differs from the description of that same occupation in another chapter--that is to be expected. In the same way, salary information may differ from chapter to chapter for the same occupational title. Keep those differences in mind as you read.

In Chapters 3-9 information is provided about seven different settings where helping professionals work. These are not all the work settings, but a representative sample of the major work setting options for counseling and human services professionals. For each chapter the following questions will be answered:

- What are the types of places in which you might work?
- Who would you be helping?
- What job responsibilities would you have in this work setting?
- What personal characteristics do you need to work in this setting?
- As a new professional, what salary might you expect?
- What education and training do you need to enter these jobs?
- What credential or license is required to work in this setting?

WORK SETTINGS

The seven work settings described help you understand the many different places where a helping professional might work.

Chapter 3: Careers in school settings. This chapter discusses the types of activities that school counselors do, such as providing one-to-one and group counseling for students, working with teachers to develop programs to improve the learning environment for students and teachers, teaching classes about subjects such as adjustment to school or career choice, or working with students about dealing with peer pressure. School counselors might work with sensitive issues such as AIDS education or might work with students who have questions about their own sexuality. Other careers in the helping professions that are frequently found in school settings are mentioned in this chapter.

Chapter 4: Careers in higher education settings. Colleges and universities, community colleges, and proprietary schools are all places where persons in the helping professions work. Careers in student services are described, such as orientation director, financial aid officer, residence hall complex coordinator, learning skills counselor, counseling center counselor, or student activities program coordinator. This is a long chapter because higher education is a complex environment where many persons are employed in many different jobs.

Chapter 5: Careers in business and industry. There are a number of different counseling and human services positions in business and industrial settings. A new and growing occupation--employee assistance program (EAP) consultant--is described in this chapter. Outplacement counselor, employment recruiter, training specialist, and substance abuse counselor are occupations included in this chapter. Common to all of these occupations is that the helping professional works in or with a business or industry.

Chapter 6: Careers in private practice. This chapter examines what type of person is well suited for a career as a private practitioner. It addresses private practice activities, including one-to-one and group counseling, consulting, and teaching-training opportunities for private practitioners who are counselors, psychologists, and social workers. Private practitioners work for themselves or with a small group of other professionals. It is a small business.

Chapter 7: Careers in federal and state agencies. Agencies that are organized or funded by states or the federal government are described in this chapter. The kinds of careers discussed in this chapter include counselors in the employment service, the military, or detention or correction facilities. Other counseling and human services careers in state and federal agencies include youth counselor, parole officer, vocational rehabilitation counselor, and correction psychologist. State and federal agencies employ persons in many different occupations.

Chapter 8: Careers in health care facilities. Nearly every community has some kind of health care facility. You will find many counseling and human services careers in the various health care facilities, including counselor, psychologist, health or wellness counselor, social worker, music or art therapist, nurse, or aides. This chapter describes many of those careers.

Chapter 9: Careers in residential treatment centers. Residential treatment centers are places where clients live during treatment. The many different residential treatment centers have opportunities for persons with education in counseling and human services. Recreation or physical therapist, rehabilitation counselor, speech-language therapist, psychologist, and case manager are a few of the occupational titles described in this chapter.

Chapter 10: Accreditation and credentialing. This chapter presents information about how preparation programs are accredited and what accreditation means to you as a prospective student. This chapter includes information about certification and licensure of helping professionals. This is important information as you examine different schools you might want to attend. Professionals in counseling and human services are frequently licensed, registered, or certified.

Chapter 11: What next? This chapter makes suggestions about the next steps that you might take in pursuing a career in counseling or human services. Some reflective exercises that will help in deciding about a career in one of these fields.

Appendix: The Appendix of this book contains names and addresses of organizations and associations related to the professions discussed in each of the chapters. At the end of most chapters will be a suggestion for "Additional Information and Resources." If you want to pursue one of the career topics, the addresses in the Appendix will be very helpful.

PREPARING TO READ THIS BOOK

Careers in the counseling and human services professions can be rewarding and exciting. They can also be frustrating and discouraging. These occupations provide many opportunities for the professional to help others grow and change throughout their life span. Human services professionals are expected to be in demand in the future. Particular demand areas include work with adults and aging people, consulting, work with outplacement and career changes, and many facets of mental health counseling. Emerging careers in the helping professions deal with new and changing social issues--working with people with AIDS, intervention programs with gang members, or counseling programs for persons who are contending with issues related to sexuality concerns.

TERMINOLOGY

In this first chapter, we have used the terms *counseling and human services* and *helping professions* to describe the fields that include all the different occupations covered in this book. Each of these terms is partially descriptive of the field and each term also limits meaning. It is difficult to find a single inclusive descriptor. Most of the professionals described do some counseling, yet not all are counselors; some, but not all, of the occupations described would be classified as professions, with rigorous preparation and licensing requirements; every occupation described in this book has something to do with people. Because people, human beings, are the focus of every occupation described in this book, we will use the term *human services* as the general descriptor for the remaining chapters. We will often use the term *counselor* to refer to a set of human service professionals.

TRENDS AND ISSUES

Several factors influence the fields of counseling and human services. The future of this relatively young field is changing--and it is difficult to predict where the greatest changes will take place. Persons who are considering a profession in one of the counseling or human services fields would be well advised to examine each of the following trends and issues to decide how they might affect their own career choices.

Changes in Health Care

Because many counselors work in systems that are supported by health care revenue, any change in the health care system affects counselors in private practice and in agency settings. In recent years, the structure of health care systems has changed, greatly affecting who is paid for service and how they are paid. States have worked to obtain licensure for counselors [see Chapter 10], only to find that health maintenance organizations (HMOs) or other care systems may change the definition of who can provide service and be paid. Changes in health care have emphasized shorter periods of treatment and treatment only for specified diagnoses. Some of these issues are discussed in Chapter 6--Careers in Private Practice. It is likely that there will be additional changes in health insurance systems as both state and federal legislation include structural reform of Medicare, Medicaid, and other forms of health care.

Demographic Changes

America is becoming a more diverse population. Changes in the population, described by changing demographic studies, indicate that there are increasing proportions of ethnic minority peoples in all urban locations. One statistic that is frequently quoted is that by the year 2010, the White American-European population in the United States will have become a numerical minority. This fact has a significant impact on all the counseling and human services professions. It is obvious that the helping professions must become more culturally diverse in their membership and more culturally sensitive in their professional practice. Other changes in the population, such as an increasing number and proportion of aging persons in the population, indicate that specialties such as gerontological counseling will become more in demand.

School Reform

Many counselors work in schools [see Chapter 3]. Schools are undergoing dramatic changes tied to three different forces: reduced funding, legislated reform, and changing student populations. The trend in educational funding over the last several years has resulted in schools having less money to spend for staff and instructional programs. The result has been reduction in numbers of specialty staff-- such as counselors--in several states. This trend is not likely to change quickly, even though Claire Cole Vaught points out in Chapter 3 that there will be a need for school counselors in the future. Educational reform measures have called for changes in the way that schools are operated, with increased demands for accountability and increased emphasis on employability of public school graduates. This means that counselors in schools will have to emphasize career development programs and be involved in school-to-work programs, particularly at the secondary level. The third trend, changing school populations, will place increased demands on counselors in schools--work with youth in gangs, increasingly diverse student populations, and youth who live in a mobile society with less certainty about employment for their parents, all have implications for professionals in schools.

A major change in the way that social services will be delivered in the future is called "integration of services." This means that social service systems will be located in the school instead of having the clients--student and or family--go to different agencies for assistance. Mental health counselors from community agencies are likely to have offices in the schools, and school counselors are likely to become more involved in the management of different service providers. Schools are becoming a place where it is common to have treatment programs for persons with alcohol and other drug problems. Some of those treatment providers may come from outside the regular school ranks.

Social Issues

In the last decade, issues such as AIDS have permeated nearly every aspect of life and professional practice. Counselors must be aware of the implication of social, political, economic, and cultural issues that affect their clients. There is no area of professional practice that will not be impacted by clients, friends, or families of people with AIDS. Similarly, counselors must be prepared to work with people who are homeless, people struggling with sexual orientation issues, clients dealing with emotional or sexual abuse, and those who planned a long career in a secure job only to find that they are unemployed and near the end of their work life. A growing trend in the counseling and human services fields is to be more of an activist in responding to issues at their source rather than to work only with the clients who are affected by social, economic, health, or political forces. For example, a counselor might work with parents of elementary school students to improve parenting skills, help children build self-esteem, and develop responses to difficult neighborhood situations to reduce the possibility that these children would be alienated from family. Alienated youth are more likely to join gangs for social support.

Technology Changes

Several chapter authors in this book have mentioned that counselors must be able to use available technology in order to do their jobs well. Keeping up with technological change is a difficult task. For counselors, the use of current technology enhances their ability to communicate with clients, to know more about client issues, and to bring the best information to client decisions. Rather than be ignorant of computer technology or be a slave to technology---whether it is a computer or a cellular phone-- counselors must be able to use technology to do their jobs better. Much of the counseling process involves bringing clients in contact with the information they need in order to make good personal decisions. Counselors who rely on antiquated methods of information access border on unethical practice in an age of rapid information access and retrieval.

Workplace Changes

The workplace is changing. The move to a service economy, with more persons employed in flexible-hour jobs and with less long-term commitment to a single employer, will demand changes of counselors who work with those employees [see Chapter 5]. The way that counselors work will also change, with fewer counselors employed for long years with the same employer and more counselors doing contract work on a part-time or limited basis. It will be common for counselors to have two, three, or four different contracts with two or more agencies that they combine to make a full-time job. Associated with this kind of work place--both for counselors and other employees--is less security of employment, less availability of health care or retirement benefits, and more change. Counselors and other human service professionals who want to be at the forefront of their professions will need to be attentive to societal changes. They must be able to expand their knowledge of their profession and of the changing world in order to provide the best care to their clients.

Chapter 2

SO YOU THINK YOU WANT A CAREER IN THE HUMAN SERVICES

Brooke B. Collison
Nancy J. Garfield

Do you think you might like a career in the field of counseling or human services? Have you known persons whose careers enable them to help people and thought you might like to do the same thing? This book will show you some of the different careers and how you might enter a career in a work setting where you are able to work with and help people.

Before you examine different work settings and learn about the occupations in each of those settings, it would be helpful for you to think about yourself and learn about personal characteristics that would be important in choosing a counseling or human services career. First, let us explain what we mean when we talk about counseling and human services careers.

COUNSELING CAREERS

Counseling careers include those professional occupations that have the word *counselor* in the job title. In general, they include occupations in which you help people in some way--either by working with them in individual sessions or in small groups. You might do that work in a private office or in one of many work settings--schools, colleges, a federal or state agencies, health care settings, or even in a business setting. Some occupations in this career field may be performed by people with other titles--psychologist, social worker, therapist, or child development specialist. We will use the term *counseling careers* to include all these occupations because they have one thing in common--they all emphasize working with people to assist them in some aspect of their life. People might need assistance with severe problems or with minor decisions; however, in each case, the

9

counseling professional does something to assist them in their particular situation.

HUMAN SERVICES CAREERS

Human services careers include many different occupations in which the professional works with people, but the job title may not include words like *counselor, psychologist, social worker, nurse, psychiatrist, marriage and family therapist, mental health professional,* or *therapist.* These careers are more frequently found in large institutions such as schools or colleges where the professional would work with people with normal, developmental issues. In these situations, people need help not so much with problems, but with every day concerns that require some kind of professional assistance. When you read Chapter 4 about careers in higher education settings, for example, you will see that some careers in higher education settings deal with financial aid, advising, housing, or job placement. These are careers in human services. Just as in counseling careers, persons in these settings work with people.

WHAT DO YOU KNOW ABOUT YOURSELF?

Before you can decide what kind of profession you want to enter, you have to know a lot of things about yourself. It is important to be willing to see yourself as human--that means having problems just like everyone else. It is important to be able to seek out and accept help with those problems. And it is important to find solutions to those problems. After all, if you enter one of the careers in counseling and human services, you will expect people to come to you with their problems, just as you should be able to take yours to someone else.

How well do you like working closely with people?

- Do you relate well with other people?
- Do you want to work with people as your major job activity?
- Do you like working with many different people?
- Do you like working with people with problems?

What work activities do you desire?

- What kind of work activities do you find exciting and rewarding?
- What kind of work activities do you think would really bore you or make you lose interest in your work?

What kind of student are you?

- If you were to make a list of your academic strengths and weaknesses, what would be on those two lists?
- How much education do you plan to acquire?

Do you have role models?

- Do you know one or more human service professionals? In what ways are you alike? Dissimilar? Do you want to be like them? Why?
- How extensive or how limited is your knowledge of the different careers available in human services? Do you know enough to make good choices among those careers?

What do you need in order to feel good about yourself?

- How do you feel when you do and don't get praise or criticism?
- What do you do when you get tired or depressed?
- Do you have the kind of good habits that maintain your health--habits such as eating well, exercising, and finding variety in your daily life?
- Do you know when you have problems and need help from others?

Do you have decision-making skills?

- Do you believe that you have good decision-making skills that would enable you to make career plans and life choices with confidence?

Do you want to work with people? Occupations are often described in terms of spending time with "data, people, or things." Nearly all careers in counseling and human services emphasize working with people. The exceptions might be a few occupations where research or information is emphasized, but the careers described in this book will most commonly describe "working with people" as a core of the job to be performed.

Do you really like to work with people? This is a serious question you must answer in making a career decision. "Working with people" means that you would be in contact with people much of the time in your job--you would listen to them talk about themselves, and hear them describe their problems; you would work with people who are upset, and you would spend time in conference with people whose lives might be unpleasant. The important question to ask yourself concerning working with people is, "Do I like to be around all kinds of people and can I maintain interest in helping them?" This is different than having many people around you who are interested in you.

Sometimes it is hard to find a good way to answer the question asked above. The question becomes even more complex when you ask yourself, "WHY do I like to help people?" If you find, for example, that you frequently spend time talking with your friends and that they often come to you with their problems, does that mean that you should enter a career in counseling or human services? That answer may come by asking yourself, "Why do my friends come to me and what do I get from helping them with their problems?" If your answer is that they come to you because you tell them what they want to hear or because you will solve their problems for them, then a career in counseling or human services may not be a good choice. If you find that you like to have them bring their problems to you because it makes you feel important or it gives you some kind of power or control over them, then a career in counseling or human services may not be a good idea. On the other hand, if people come to you because (a) you are a good listener, (b) you remain impartial and objective, and (c) you help them figure out what to do but you don't feel they should solve their problems exactly the same way you would, then a career in counseling or human services might be a good choice for you.

What about your own problems? Do you think that you should be free of personal problems to enter a counseling or human services career? Or do you think that the only way to help people would be to have had a similar problem and have solved it yourself? Persons who think about entering careers in counseling and human services frequently express each of these ideas. You don't have to be problem-free in order to enter the helping professions. On the other hand, you should not go into the counseling profession just to straighten out your own life. As a helping professional it is important to remember that:

- all people have problems;
- no two people have the same problems;
- counselors are people;
- counselors have problems;
- a counselor and a client might have similar but not identical problems; and
- counselors need help with their own problems in the same way that other people need help with theirs.

If people who enter careers in counseling and human services believe that they should not have problems or that they should not reveal their problems to other professionals, they are forcing themselves into an unhealthy situation. They are presuming to help others or to ask others to seek help when they are unwilling to do the same for themselves; therefore, we suggest that it is important for the counselor to acknowledge that problems do exist and be able to seek help for those problems. We are also saying that it is not necessary to have had a particular problem in order to help people with that problem. You do not have to be a child of an alcoholic family in order to help children of alcoholic families; you do not have to be divorced to help people who are divorced; you don't have to have lost a parent in order to help others who have had a parent die. At the same time, if you are a child of an alcoholic family, you might have some insight into the concerns of persons from an alcoholic family, but their experiences area still different from your own, and to assume that they are the same is not a good basis for working with other people.

Another important issue to examine concerning the helping professions and your own problem history is connected to problem solutions. Sometimes a person who has solved a problem wants to become a helping professional so that everyone with a similar problem will adopt the same solution. They can become fanatical about having other people "do what they did" to stop smoking, get off drugs, make their marriage better, or go to the same college they attended. These are not good counseling approaches. They are not good reasons for going into the counseling or human services professions.

Rewarding work activities. Do you ever fantasize about an ideal job? What things make you feel good about your work--whether at school, in a job, or at home? Do you need to see immediate, tangible results of your work in order to feel good about it, or can you work on a project and never know how it will come out, perhaps not even getting credit for your work even if it does work out well? Can you work in the background and enjoy the fruits of your labor, or do you have to be right out in front getting the applause?

In many human services careers it is difficult to know if your work is successful. Sometimes your success may not be known for a long time--perhaps several years. There are instances where a person you might work with will be successful, but you won't know whether their success was due to something you did or a combination of other factors. In addition, counselors work privately and confidentially with clients--if success is achieved in some activity, clients aren't likely to stand up and give public credit to the counselor who helped them if telling that means that they reveal something that is private and personal.

People change very slowly. Some problems that counselors and others work with are difficult to change. For example, people who work in prisons often talk about the "recidivism rate"--the rate at which persons who are released from jail return because they haven't changed their offending behaviors. The same problems exist for counselors who work with alcohol or other drug abusers--clients may complete a treatment program and seem to be "cured," but in a short time after their completion of the program, many may be using alcohol or other drugs again. This can be discouraging for counselors who work with such persons. Do you think that you would be able to feel good about your own work if the signs of success were few and far between? Could you have a sense of accomplishment or be satisfied with your job if only 1 out of 10 people you worked with was "successful"?

The rewarding side of a career in the counseling or human services field comes when you see people you have worked with solve a personal problem, make a decision that you both know is a good one, or develop good feelings about themselves. When the person you have been working with reaches a point where your services are no longer needed, it can be a good feeling--one that you will know about but may not be able to share with others. In many counseling situations, you may never know the outcome of your work.

JOB SATISFACTION

People are best suited for counseling and human services careers if they can be satisfied to (a) know they have done the best they can do, (b) judge their jobs for themselves, (c) be patient with outcomes, (d) accept that progress will occur in small steps, and (e) work in situations they cannot control. The salaries for persons in counseling careers range from very low for part-time professionals to very high for highly skilled consultants or persons in executive positions. Most human service occupations will pay moderate wages, and people who require a high salary or income tend not to enter these occupations.

How do you react to the problems you encounter in your own life? Can you see them as situations that can be resolved to your advantage? Can you seek help with the problems you have? Do you have a circle of friends with whom you can share your concerns and from whom you know that you would get understanding and support? Do you have a good sense of your own values and beliefs and know enough about yourself that you could be confronted with conflicting values and not be upset? If you can answer "Yes" to the last four questions, you are a good candidate for a career in counseling and human services professions.

Are you a good student? Nearly all human service careers require undergraduate and graduate study. You will see in the chapters that follow that some careers demand more education than others, but graduate degrees are common for most. What kind of student are you? A majority of the course work for careers in the helping professions will emphasize reading, writing, and verbal skills. In addition, specialized study in counseling and human services professions will include course work in several of the behavioral sciences--psychology, sociology, or anthropology--as well as course work in statistics and research methodology. Acceptance to graduate study for the majors in these fields will require good performance on undergraduate studies in addition to other admission criteria.

The academic courses that have high relevance to careers in counseling and human services are the language arts--written and oral expression; social and behavioral sciences; mathematics--especially statistics; and academic activities where you have social interaction. The academic emphasis would be on interactions with people, understanding people, written and analytical thinking--helping people solve problems, and being able to feel confident about yourself in those interactions.

The amount of education required will depend on which career field you explore. You will find that you can enter some careers in counseling and human services with an undergraduate education. Most will require a graduate degree--at least a master's degree--and some will require a doctoral degree. Some careers in counseling and human services may require advanced training or an internship (an extensive supervised counseling experience) in addition to a doctoral degree. An internship may be necessary before or after completion of a degree, and represents a significant amount of supervised time spent in professional work.

Who are your models? Do you know people who are professionals in one of the counseling or human services careers? Watching and talking with people can be helpful in learning what they do, how they got in to their field, what they like and dislike about it, and whether they would enter the same field again if they had the opportunity to do so. Frequently, people may want to enter a field because they have been helped by a professional and they decide that they would like to be just like that person. This is not a bad reason for choosing a field if your characteristics match those necessary for that career. Choosing a career just because you had a good experience with a particular counselor or advisor is not a good reason in itself to make such an important decision.

Another common reason people want to enter one of the helping professions is that they have or have had a particular problem or situation in their own life and they want to see other people solve it in a similar way. This is not a good reason for choosing a career unless you have truly worked through all the aspects of the problem issue, and you have other reasons for making that career choice.

It would be a good idea to know several persons in a profession before deciding that should be your career. Knowing only one professional person in a counseling or human services occupation provides a limited view of the career field.

Your career decision-making skills. How good are your own decision-making skills? There are few decisions that you will make in your life that are as significant as, "What are you going to do for your life's work?" If you have studied career decisions, you know that few people make one decision early in life and then enter an occupation and remain there until they retire. It is more likely that you will change your mind several times about what you are going to do before you actually enter your profession. After entering a profession, other kinds of changes may be natural or logical--changes such as advancement through the stages of a career in what might be called a "career ladder." Other career changes may be more unexpected, as you decide to leave a profession all together and do something else with your life. Frequently, success in one area may lead to possibilities in a different occupation. Each of those changes is a critical point along the career development path. Each requires critical decision-making ability.

How do you make decisions now? Do you gather information, consider alternatives, think about consequences, and then make careful steps toward implementation? Or do you listen to other people and try to do what they want you to do rather than what you would want yourself? Do you move quickly into new decisions without much thought of the past and the future, or do you take a long time to think and plan before you act?

It is important for you to think about your decision-making style and then apply that knowledge to make a career decision. Make a list of some of the major and minor decisions you have made in the past several years. After you have listed those decisions, think about how you made them. Apply the questions found above to the decisions you listed. How many of the decisions do you look back on as "good" decisions, and how many are decisions that you would like to have the opportunity to do over? Can you draw any conclusions from that about how you should look at decisions that are as important as entering a career in the counseling or human services professions, or in any other career area for that matter?

MOVING AHEAD

Are you ready to move ahead? Here is a check list of questions you might ask yourself. Make a copy of that check list and use it as a book mark while you read through this book. At the end of your reading, review the items on the check list again as you consider your career decisions.

Yes No   *Questions for Myself*

__ __   Do I want to work with people as my major job activity?
__ __   Do I like different kinds of people?
__ __   Can I accept help from others for my own problems?
__ __   I like to help other people with their problems.
__ __   I would like to work in an office setting.
__ __   I would like to work alone.
__ __   Written and verbal activities are interesting.
__ __   I am a good student, particularly in language arts and social and behavioral sciences.
__ __   I can describe my own academic strengths and weaknesses.
__ __   I plan to earn a college degree and have thought about going on to graduate school.
__ __   I know more than one person in the counseling or human services field.
__ __   I am able to make good decisions for myself.

Good wishes as you move ahead.

Chapter 3

CAREERS IN SCHOOL SETTINGS

Claire Cole Vaught

If you are a fifteen-year-old high school student, to whom can you talk if you:

- are panic stricken that you are pregnant?
- wonder how to study to become an osteopath?
- think your auto mechanics teacher is picking on you because you are the only girl in class?
- believe your best friend is becoming an alcoholic?
- worry that you might fail English and not graduate?
- have a chance at a prestigious academic scholarship and want help getting recommendations and writing an essay?
- cannot stand your biology teacher one minute longer?
- need a job but can't read the job application to fill it out?

If you were a twelve-year-old middle school student, to whom could you go if you:

- worry because you are 3 inches shorter than everyone else in your class?
- think your best friends of last year are immature and silly but don't want to give them up and be friendless?
- fear that your parents are getting a divorce?
- worry you might have AIDS because you sat next to a boy who looks really sick?
- know that your best friend is shoplifting?
- want to graduate from high school in 3 years instead of 4 and don't know if that's possible?
- love your clarinet and wonder if there's some summer camp in music you could attend?
- need to earn money because your mother just lost her job?

If you were an eight-year-old elementary student, who could help you if you:

- feel sick to your stomach every morning before you go to school?
- want to be a professional football player but your mother won't let you go out for sandlot football?
- think writing stories is great and want to learn more about that?
- hate your brother because he's so mean to you?
- have a pain in your back where your father hit you when he came home drunk last night?
- can't sleep because you hear gunshots in your dreams from when your cousin was shot last summer?
- don't know how to stay out of fights in the playground?
- live in a homeless shelter and know nothing about this new school?

The answer to whom you could go to for help in finding answers to all these questions is your school counselor. There are many people in a school who help students: teachers, principals, librarians, and others. While these people often assist students with their personal concerns, their primary job is something else: teaching, running the school, and managing media. The school counselor's primary job is helping students handle whatever personal concerns keep them from learning the best they can, as well as helping young people plan for future education and careers.

WHERE DO SCHOOL COUNSELORS WORK?

School counselors work with students from about the ages of 4 through 18 in primary, elementary, intermediate, middle, junior high, and high schools. Occasionally counselors work with students younger than 4, such as in preschool and other programs for disabled or at-risk children that may begin as early as 2 years of age. And sometimes they work with postgraduate students older than 18 who are still attending high schools.

Most high schools and middle/junior high schools in the U.S. have school counselors. To be accredited--that is, be recognized as good schools--high schools must provide counseling services. In some states, the number of students one high school counselor can be assigned is suggested by the state. A ratio of 250:1 would mean that a counselor would be responsible for 250 students. Thus, a high school of 1,000 students would have four counselors. The number is usually higher for middle/junior high--perhaps 400:1; and for elementary-- maybe 500:1. This means that middle or elementary school counselors are likely to have very high numbers of students assigned to them, making it more difficult for them to provide services for individual counselees.

There are also school counselors in some other countries, including Israel and Canada, but the school counselor is more of an American tradition. Counselors who want to go to another country often work in Department of Defense schools with dependents of American military personnel.

School counselors usually have an office in the school building, or perhaps a small classroom or conference room where groups of students come for different kinds of activities. Often a counseling office suite includes space for visitors to sit while they wait for the counselor, a secretary's work space, storage space (sometimes a vault) for records and other materials, and a conference room where groups of people can meet.

School counselors occasionally go to a student's home or to businesses or other schools in the community. If counselors are appointed to school district committees, they may have to attend meetings outside the school building.

WITH WHOM DO SCHOOL COUNSELORS WORK?

School counselors are a part of the team of people working in the school. They work closely with teachers and administrators to help their counselees. Often elementary and middle school counselors teach guidance lessons in the classroom, team teaching with the regular classroom teacher. Counselors consult with teachers when a student is having difficulty and often include parents in the consultation. School principals seek counselors' help to plan programs and to identify ways to improve the school so that students can learn better. Counselors also work with educational specialists: nurses, social workers, gifted specialists, homebound teachers, psychologists, special education personnel, and others who help individual students. Mental health professionals from the community often seek school counselors' views of their school-aged clients. Parental permission is required whenever information is shared with a psychiatrist, probation worker, social services worker, court services person, psychologist, or other mental health professional.

It is becoming common in some communities for a variety of social service agencies to work together--often at the school site. In some instances, this system is referred to as "integrated services" or "school-linked social service." Regardless of what it is called, it requires new functions of the school counselor who perhaps will function as a coordinator of various service providers--social workers, psychologists, child protective service workers, probation officers, workers from family aid programs, and other public agency or private service systems. The school counselor may become less the person who provides service to students in school and more the person who coordinates a variety of services from numerous community agencies.

WHOM DO SCHOOL COUNSELORS HELP?

School counseling differs from many other mental health professions because school counselors work with the entire student population, most of whom are psychologically healthy. They do not just see students with problems who need therapeutic counseling; rather, they provide personal, educational, and career counseling for all students. They may also, through classroom guidance, provide information for all students on how people develop normally, describing some common feelings, worries, and fears that most students in an age group encounter. Although school counselors work with parents, teachers, and other adults who surround the student, the counselor's primary client is always the student. The school counselor is--first and foremost--a student advocate.

WHAT DOES A SCHOOL COUNSELOR DO?

A counselor's day in a high school can be very different from one in an elementary school, but all counselors do certain things, including counsel with individuals or groups of students who want to change some aspect of their behavior such as make better grades, get along better with parents, or make new friends. They consult with parents, teachers, principals, mental health professionals, and others who deal with students. Counselors provide information on a variety of topics, depending on the age of the counselees, from describing community helpers for kindergarten students to helping high school seniors understand the college application process. Counselors interpret tests and collect other kinds of information needed to help students do good planning and move to the next level of preparation for education and career.

An elementary counselor's day might go something like this: Meet with parents and teacher to enroll a new student. Visit three second-grade classrooms and conduct classroom guidance lessons on how to handle anger. Plan a program for all students on "good touch, bad touch" to teach about sexual abuse. Have a group counseling session for four fifth graders having trouble keeping friends. See three students by individual appointment who were referred by their teachers. Attend a staff meeting and help develop an individualized plan for a special education student needing counseling services. Often, an elementary counselor serves more than one school, so the schedule may be condensed while the counselor moves to another school around midday; or, the counselor may be in one school certain days of the week and in another school on alternating days.

A middle school counselor's day might be a little different. It could include the following activities or events: Attend a parent conference with sixth-grade team teachers before school. Supervise teacher advisory activity during homeroom period, when teachers deliver classroom group guidance to all students throughout the school. Counsel three individuals by appointment: one new student having trouble adjusting; one girl who has boyfriend problems; and one boy who gets into fights. Conduct two group counseling sessions on growing into adolescence, which every seventh grader attends. Attend a seventh-grade team meeting to discuss students about whom teachers are worried. Meet with high school counselors to plan a visit to the high school for eighth graders. In between these activities, the middle school counselor might have made several phone calls to a community agency in an effort to arrange weekly in-school visits from therapists who will be working with a group of children identified for some particular issue.

The high school counselor's day will be similar to the middle school counselor's, with a few different twists. The list of possible activities might include the following: Review computer printouts to be sure seniors are passing the classes they need to graduate. Meet with a college representative who wants to leave information about her school. Counsel six students by appointment: college admissions questions, where to get a job, trouble getting along with a parent, fear of pregnancy, general unhappiness and lack of motivation, and schedule problem. Discuss plans with the principal for the annual College and Career Night. Arrange for a counseling group on substance abuse to be conducted by an outside agency.

All three counselors--elementary, middle, and high school--use the same skills of establishing a relationship with the student, identifying a problem or concern, planning ways to make changes in the student's way of behaving, evaluating progress, and following up with the student to be sure things continue to go well. But the topics and the techniques used vary greatly as counselors do different things in different ways with younger and older students. All three would spend time with agencies and organizations outside the school as part of their efforts to bring needed social services in to the school site.

Computer skills make a counselor's life easier. Computer data management is required of counselors. Schedules, other school records, career and educational information, and other data bases are important to a school counselor. While many counselors have a clerical assistant, they should know how to use a computer to work more efficiently.

WHAT AFFECTS A SCHOOL COUNSELOR'S WORK?

Because education is a public business, politics plays a part in the school counselor's job. Budget cuts may, for example, mean fewer counselors if the community sees counseling as "non-essential." Community groups may have a strong say in what services are offered; conservative religious groups may object to what they see as "mind-altering" techniques used by the school counselor. In some schools, the counselor may work with the family life program; in others, virtually any mention of subjects such as abortion or birth control is taboo. Since education is a state responsibility, it is possible for state legislatures to pass laws that would require school counselors to do certain tasks--meeting with every student to develop educational plans, or assuring that each student had a signed career plan on file. State legislatures can pass laws that change school requirements and subsequently change the counselor's job.

WHAT ARE SCHOOL COUNSELORS LIKE AS PEOPLE?

School counselors like students and know how to talk to younger people. Not only must they have the skills of any other mental health professional, they must be able to establish rapport with young people to make students trust and believe in them. They typically have a genuine interest in students and are often the best adult "cheerleaders" students have--they must be able to establish rapport and then have the counseling skills to help students achieve their goals. Counselors who work in schools must get along with adults, because they work on a team; whereas, a teacher may be able to work behind a closed classroom door, a counselor is in the mainstream of school life, working with virtually every individual in the building, both adult and student. Counselors must also be able to organize well, because they see many students in a short period of time, return a seemingly infinite number of phone calls, and help plan many programs and activities. They must be ingenious thinkers because there are few rules for human behavior: different solutions must be tried with different individuals. They must also have good judgment and common sense. As spokespersons for the school, they need to be correct and sensible. As observers of people, they must have good understanding of human behavior and make good decisions. A missed cue may mean a suicide, a drug overdose, or a school dropout. Counselors must have excellent human relations skills, because they meet many angry and upset people.

Because counselors are often called upon in a crisis, they must have a high energy level, be able to remain calm, and think quickly and clearly. If there is a suicide in a school, for example, a counselor must be able to function as a part of a crisis team without collapsing due to personal emotion. School counseling is a demanding but rewarding job for those who are able to work on a team, enjoy being around young people, and identify and use resources outside the school.

Counselors in schools must accept all kinds of people who are different from themselves: economic, racial, ethnic, gender, and lifestyle differences. School counselors cannot pick and choose who their clients will be; they work with everyone assigned to them in a school. They must be tolerant of views different from theirs, and must know enough about other cultures to at least not offend their clients. Schools typically have very diverse populations; counselors must take great care not to work only with those students from backgrounds like their own, with familiar values and aspirations.

HOW MUCH MONEY DO SCHOOL COUNSELORS EARN?

Usually the pay for school counselors is based on a teacher's salary scale, although sometimes the director of counseling in a school is considered an administrator. Because they have master's degrees and often work more days than do teachers, they may have salary supplements that teachers do not receive. There is a great range of teaching salaries within the U.S.A., but a beginning counselor with a master's degree can expect to earn more than $20,000 a year.

HOW DO YOU BECOME A SCHOOL COUNSELOR?

Most school counselors have been teachers before they became counselors and have an undergraduate (bachelor's degree) in an area such as English, vocational education, or elementary education. In some states, teaching is not a prerequisite for a school counseling job. People who want to be school counselors attend a university to study individual and group counseling theories and techniques; consultation; career and educational information; testing and measurement; working with special populations such as minorities, the gifted, and special education students; and other courses. The program may also include courses on families, substance abuse, and other special topics. Counselors complete a practicum or internship--supervised practice in a school working under the supervision of an experienced school counselor--before they complete a master's degree.

There usually is specific course work and practicum experience for the level at which the counselor will be endorsed to work--high, middle, or elementary school. Each state sets its own requirements for being a school counselor. If a person who wants to be a counselor meets those requirements, he or she is said to be "certified" or "endorsed" or "licensed" to be a school counselor.

Most states require additional training to keep the endorsement up-to-date. The profession is constantly changing as people find new and better ways to help their counselees, and as new topics become important for counselors to understand. A few years ago, school counselors did not know about anorexia or AIDS; now they must know about such problems in society. Counselors also keep themselves up-to-date by reading journals such as *The School Counselor* and *Elementary School Guidance and Counseling.* They attend conferences sponsored by state and local branches of the American Counseling Association (ACA) and its affiliate for school counselors, the American School Counseling Association (ASCA).

LEARNING MORE ABOUT BEING A SCHOOL COUNSELOR

There are several good ways to learn more about school counseling:

1. The best source of information on school counseling will be counselors currently working in schools. They like to share information with students who are interested in becoming school counselors, and they will know what is required in that state to be credentialed as a school counselor.

2. Another source of information is the *Occupational Outlook Handbook* (OOH), which is almost surely in the school guidance office. Other similar publications give information on school counseling as a profession.

3. There may be a computerized career information service, such as the state's occupational information system, that is found in many school counseling offices or in some public libraries. A computerized information service will give information on where to study counseling in a particular state and perhaps some employment outlook trends for that region.

4. Universities with a graduate program in counseling are another good source of information. Professors in counselor education can tell prospective students about what kind of preparation program is involved, as well as entrance requirements.

5. Professional organizations such as ACA and ASCA have state and local affiliates. They welcome a student visitor who is a prospective counselor.

WHAT IS THE FUTURE FOR SCHOOL COUNSELING?

In most states, there seems to be a bright future for school counselors. Although there have been some cutbacks in school counseling programs due to reductions in funding for special services, many states are putting emphasis on the kinds of services school counselors offer. As more attention is paid to individuals through special education and programs for the gifted, more information and support are needed at the school level for students. Dropout intervention is a current concern for many educators and legislators; school counselors are likely to be involved in dropout programs. As American society believes in individual choice and has the affluence to provide the means to help individuals make wise choices, the school counselor will figure importantly in schools to help students see their options in life and plan programs to get them there. Societal concerns such as AIDS, substance abuse, minority concerns, gang activity, and others means that someone has to pay attention to the individual youth growing up--and often that "someone" is the school counselor.

Another important trend in school counseling is the emphasis on counseling for all students, including those at the middle- and elementary-school level. Increasingly, counselors are being added in those areas, making a whole new cadre of counselors necessary, just as many counselors trained in the 1950s and 1960s are retiring. The trend to have school counselors work with different social service agencies in bringing assistance to students and families requires a strong set of organizational skills on the part of the counselor.

OTHER HELPING PROFESSIONALS IN THE SCHOOL

Many school principals and teachers have some training in basic counseling skills and are very willing and able to help students with their personal concerns. School psychologists and school social workers have training similar to that of school counselors, but have different responsibilities within the school system. Much of their time is spent with the evaluation required for students receiving special education services. The school psychologist is skilled in administering and interpreting tests, especially tests that measure characteristics related to students' success in school. They counsel parents, students, and teachers about factors that influence a student's achievement.

School psychologists often provide consultation for teachers regarding students with learning or behavior problems, and some do individual or group counseling with students. Usually a school psychologist serves several schools, or may be a professional outside the school system hired specifically to do special psychological or educational evaluations.

The school social worker works between the school and the home to help students do well in school. Often the school social worker has responsibility for trying to get students to school when they are poor attenders. The social worker also helps families find the help they need from social service agencies. Some social workers have a great deal of training in counseling, especially family counseling or therapy. Others have primarily attendance officer qualifications. There are not as many regulations about the qualifications or case load for school social workers as there are for school counselors or school psychologists.

As a result of violence in society, many schools today have police officers who work in the building every day, or who come to school regularly for programs such as DARE (Drug Abuse Resistance Education). These police officers have training as helping persons and want to prevent trouble by helping people solve their problems, not having to arrest them later. Often they are a valuable help to the counseling staff. Some schools employ specially trained counselors for particular problems such as student drug abuse.

ADDITIONAL INFORMATION AND RESOURCES

Your school counselor or a counselor at a career center can give you additional information about careers in school settings. You could also browse through the journals for school counselors--*The School Counselor,* and *Elementary School Guidance and Counseling.* The following associations can provide specific information also. Their addresses are in *Appendix A: Organizations and Associations* of this book.

American Counseling Association
American Psychological Association
American School Counselor Association
National Association of School Psychologists

National Association of School Social Workers
National Association of Social Workers

The following books can be helpful in understanding more about counseling and human services careers in schools:

Cole, C. (1988). *Guidance in Middle Schools.* Columbus, OH: National Middle School Association.
Muro, J. & Kottman, T. (1995). *Guidance and Counseling in the Elementary and Middle Schools.* Madison, WI: Wm. C. Brown Communications, Inc.
Vanzandt, C. & Hayslip, J. (1994). *Your Comprehensive School Guidance and Counseling Programs.* New York: Longman.

Chapter 4

STUDENT AFFAIRS AND RELATED CAREERS IN HIGHER EDUCATION

Susan R. Komives
Linda K. Gast

Sara Johnson slowly wakes up, stretches, and begins thinking of her busy day ahead. She loves being a junior at State University. She has to remember to see Dean Marshall about final plans for Diversity Awareness Week on her way to economics class. She needs to see a financial aid counselor to check into her application for loans and the Career Center sent her a notice that the applications for Summer internships were due Friday so she needs to get her academic advisor's signature. She has to remember to go to that workshop the Counseling Center is doing on "Helping Friends who have Eating Disorders" before work in the Admissions Office. She has a Resident Assistant staff meeting tonight at 9 after her last class. She gets her roommate, Marissa, up early so she can make it to her study skills class in the Learning Assistance Center. At breakfast, Sara says, "You know, Marissa, it just hit me that there are people all over campus who have terrific jobs and get to help students in lots of ways. I think I'd like to do that too!" Later, at the Career Center she learns that there are over 3,700 colleges and universities in the United States serving more than 13 million students every year. Every one of these institutions has from 10-300 staff working with counseling, developing, advising, and teaching students.

Higher education is big business. Helping professionals are employed in a variety of jobs and functions in colleges. Career opportunities may be found in every sector of the college--student affairs, academic affairs, and administrative offices. Most helping professionals in higher education provide services to students and are members of student affairs staffs. Some serve students within an academic department or college, such as academic advising, engineering cooperative education, or centers for women and minorities in science. Helping professionals in higher education also may assist faculty and staff through such functions as human resources or personnel, staff development and training, employment counseling, and employee assistance programs.

Student affairs staff work with students individually, in groups, and in campus communities, such as residence halls. They work in partnership with teaching faculty and other campus administrators to help students have a personally and academically successful college experience. Student affairs professionals are concerned with the development of the whole person: the intellectual, occupational, cultural, physical, emotional, social, and spiritual development of students.

Student affairs professionals help students have a productive college experience and achieve personal and academic success. They work in areas such as admissions, career development, personal counseling, student activities, academic advising, religious services, and athletics. These professionals help students living on campus or commuting to campus, provide services for special student needs, such as helping those with disabilities, and provide programs for special groups: women, ethnic students, and older adults. They educate students in classes on career and life planning; provide leadership programs, campus activities, cultural and recreational programs; and hold students accountable to community standards through judicial systems. These helping professionals need many skills including counseling, advising, consulting, teaching, assessing, administering, researching, leading, managing, and program planning.

While student affairs professionals are employed in almost all of the common helping professions (psychologist, social worker, counselor, consultant, etc.), job titles are more specific. Academic advisor, health educator, training and development specialist, career counselor, disability support services counselor, internship coordinator, and fraternity and sorority advisor are just a few of the entry job titles of helping professionals in higher education. Experienced helping professionals may be deans of students, vice presidents of student affairs, assistant or associate deans for student services, and directors of admissions, career services, counseling centers, multi cultural centers, and other student affairs offices.

INSTITUTIONAL DIVERSITY

Higher education is the broad name used for many sectors of training and education beyond high school. American higher education is diverse, including at least three primary categories of institutions:

- community and junior colleges,
- four year colleges, and
- universities.

Generally, community or junior colleges are 2-year institutions offering associate of arts (AA) degrees, certificate programs, and continuing education courses. They offer students several educational choices including college transfer programs for those preparing to go on to 4-year degrees; and vocational or occupational training programs preparing students for immediate jobs, such as air conditioning service technician, nurses aide, or dental technician. These colleges emphasize quality teaching and a concern for student development, often with an emphasis on the older adult learner. There also are 2-year schools, for upper-division students only, where students transfer from other institutions at the junior year. Four year colleges are typically small (under 3,000 students) and often are focused on the liberal arts. Students enroll to earn a bachelor's degree and many pursue graduate study after graduation. These colleges are frequently residential. Universities offer both the bachelor of arts (BA) and bachelor of science (BS); graduate degrees, such as master of arts (MA), master of science (MS), master of education (MEd), master of business administration (MBA); doctor of philosophy (PhD), doctor of education (EdD); and various professional degrees, such as those in medicine (MD), law (JD or LLD), and dentistry (DDS). Universities value faculty research and the advancement of knowledge and expect good teaching; they offer strong student affairs programs yet their large size makes it difficult to provide personal contact with each student.

Within each of these three primary categories is additional diversity. An institution may be primarily residential (students live on campus in residence halls) or totally commuter (students live at home or in apartments and travel to campus); rural or urban; public or private; non-selective (many students who apply may be admitted) or very selective (a small portion of applicants can enroll); religious or secular; primarily liberal arts or vocational; quite large (50,000 students) or very small (350 students); and financially healthy or financially struggling. Some colleges have a very special focus, for example, military schools, women's colleges, historically Black colleges, or seminaries. The characteristics of each college and the mission of that college create distinctions in the work environment. (NOTE: for ease in reading this chapter, the term "college" is used to describe all higher education institutions.)

THE STUDENTS

College students are usually high school graduates who range in age from late teens to older adult learners and senior citizens. Increasing numbers of adults in their 30s and 40s are returning for a college degree. Men and women are equally represented in most institutions, although overall, a slightly larger number of women are enrolled. Students are very diverse and campus communities include students from many racial and ethnic groups, international students, and students with various disabilities. Although most students attend full time, increasing numbers of students enroll part time, taking longer to complete their degree because of the need to work for financial support or to meet family obligations. Most college students are very motivated and often want help with their personal growth to ensure their college success.

WHY WORK IN HIGHER EDUCATION?

Rewards abound in working with college students. The traditional college student (ages 18-22) is in an exciting transition from the family environment to the interdependence of becoming an adult. Older college students are enjoying the learning they might not have been able to pursue at a younger age. They often are making career changes or seeking professional advancement and see further education as essential to these goals. Except for the occasional student who feels pressured to go to college and might not want to be there, most students want to succeed and readily work with helping professionals and faculty to learn and grow. For the most part, the issues that students bring to helping professionals are developmental in nature, although students also may seek help for such problems as abuse, chemical dependency, and suicidal thoughts.

Whatever the type of college, higher education institutions are exciting work environments. Day-to-day life might include concerts and plays, controversial speakers, breakthrough scientific discoveries, athletic events, and international food festivals. Staff and faculty colleagues are highly educated and function as professionals with autonomy, yet enjoy working together to solve problems in committees and task forces.

Staff in these settings are usually salaried employees with benefits, such as health plans, paid vacation, and retirement programs. An additional benefit at some schools is allowing the staff member and dependents some tuition-free credits at that institution. So, working in college settings means:

- motivated students who respond to help;
- meaningful work that makes a difference in students' lives;
- exciting work environments;
- highly educated colleagues; and
- good benefits.

Preparing for Student Affairs and Other Helping Professions

Most positions in student affairs require counseling and human services graduate degrees. Student affairs functions also include some specialties that require their own professional credentials. For example, the college health service would hire physicians and nurses; campus safety and security would hire law enforcement specialists; the chaplain would be an ordained clergy member; and food services would hire dieticians, nutritionists, and hotel and restaurant administration professionals.

Most entry level or beginning Student Affairs positions require at least a master's degree (MA, MS, or MEd) in one of several majors: guidance and counseling, college student development, or higher education administration. Common doctoral degrees (EdD or PhD) include college counseling, counselor education, counseling psychology, college student personnel administration, or higher education administration. Although undergraduate degrees in psychology or other behavioral sciences are desirable for some majors, such as counseling, most college student personnel and higher education administration programs will consider many different undergraduate majors. Depending on the particular graduate program, graduate study includes courses on counseling theory, counseling assessment, developmental theories of late adolescence and adults, career and group counseling, understanding the college environment, administrative and management issues, history of higher education, and higher education law. Some positions require a specialist degree while others prefer a broad, generalist background.

Begin Preparing as a College Student

Undergraduate college students can explore their interest in student affairs positions in many ways. Paid paraprofessional positions that provide intensive training and close professional supervision include (a) resident assistants who live on a residence hall floor and plan programs, develop community, handle discipline, and advise residents; (b) peer advisors who work in the counseling center, multi cultural center, or career center in special programs or work with individual students providing tutoring, academic advising, and learning assistance; and (c) student employees who work in student affairs offices. Many students gain volunteer experiences on and off campus as (a) leaders in student government, clubs, organizations, church groups, community service, sports, student union programming, and campus media; or (b) orientation peer advisors, first-year student mentors, crises hot line workers, multi cultural advisors, or members of student advisory boards for various offices. Many colleges offer experiential learning or independent study credit for these experiences. On some campuses students can sign up for special programs like leadership retreats or women's awareness symposia or enroll for credit in leadership, health education, community service, or peer advising courses.

STUDENT AFFAIRS AND OTHER HELPING FUNCTIONS

Most colleges are organized into three major units: (a) the curriculum (the academic program), (b) the co-curriculum (support services for students and experiences that aid their development outside of the classroom and success inside the classroom), and (c) administration (payroll, personnel, building maintenance, etc.).

Student affairs functions encompass the entire co-curriculum and many services for students are located in academic units as well. In addition, some helping professionals work in offices that aid faculty and staff on campus.

On small campuses faculty may provide academic advising and one office might handle many functions, such as orientation, student activities, and leadership development. In large universities one function, like student activities, could have a dozen or more full time staff. Some functions may not exist at all in some kinds of colleges; for example, most community colleges do not have residence halls. On large campuses, academic advising and other student support services may be located within academic units, like colleges of arts and sciences or education, and prefer advisors with academic majors from that college.

STUDENT AFFAIRS AND RELATED CAREERS

Helping professionals work in many different areas. Student affairs functions that require other specialties (for example, campus safety, religious life, or medical personnel in health centers) are not reviewed in this section. For each of the functional areas the following information is included: (a) examples of responsibilities, (b) nature of work, (c) qualifications, and (d) common job titles.

Salaries differ greatly among types of institutions and levels of positions; however, some salary information has been provided from a comparative salary review in *The Chronicle of Higher Education*. Generally, staff with doctorates earn more than those with master's degrees. Depending on the type of campus and previous experience, deans or vice presidents of student affairs may earn $40,000 to $95,000; directors of major programs may earn $30,000 to $80,000; entry level staff earn from the low to mid-$20s. Average salary for all types of institutions is included where available, but refers generally to upper management positions.

Academic Support Services and Academic Advising

Responsibilities: Academic support services include such diverse functions as academic advising, learning skills centers, academic tutoring services, and special clinics, like writing laboratories. In academic advising centers, staff work with individual students to plan class schedules to meet college requirements, including courses for their majors. Learning skill centers conduct individual and group sessions on time management, study skills, learning styles, effective note taking, as well as coordinate tutoring programs. Special programs may exist for student athletes, students returning to college after many years (often called re-entry services), low-achieving students, highly able students completing several majors concurrently or in honors programs, those for whom English is a second language (ESOL), and under-prepared students. **Nature of work:** These specialists work with students individually and in small groups over extended periods of time. Some students may be required to participate in these services as a condition of their enrollment, but most voluntarily seek services to improve their academic skills. **Qualifications:** Staff in these programs are usually counselors with a master's degree and special training about learning differences and skills. **Common job titles:** Director or Assistant Director of Academic Advising, Academic Advisor, Director or Assistant Director of Learning Skills Center, Coordinator of Special Services, Learning Skills Specialist. (Average salaries: Academic Advisor: $28,822).

Administration and Leadership of Student Affairs

Responsibilities: The senior student affairs officer (SSAO) supervises all student affairs departments and functions, often working with or through other department heads, and interacting with faculty, parents, alumni and community members. The SSAO is responsible for staffing, budgeting, planning, implementing policy and procedures and representing students interests with academic and business affairs administrators. This person commonly serves on the college president's cabinet and, in some institutions, may report to a provost or executive vice president. **Nature of work:** The senior student affairs officer works with staff and student leaders, and mediates student conflict and crisis situations. On larger campuses, the SSAOs work primarily with staff; on smaller campuses they may provide direct services to students. **Qualifications:** This senior level position requires extensive successful job experience and usually a doctoral degree. A graduate degree in college student personnel, student development, or higher education administration is preferred. **Common job titles:** Vice President, Vice Chancellor or Dean of Students (Average salary: Vice President $65,446; Dean of Students $52,211.)

Admission, Registration, and Enrollment Management

Responsibilities: Admissions involves identifying, attracting and admitting students qualified to enroll at the college. This function includes recruitment, screening, conducting interviews, evaluating academic transcripts, visiting secondary school guidance officers, participating in college night fairs, designing publications (videos, catalogs, and view books), and communicating with large numbers of applicants. On small college campuses, admissions may report to the president. Special functions include enrollment management to retain registered students and to recruit special populations, such as African American students. Beginning jobs usually require travel to recruit and may involve regional, national and international travel. Once students are admitted, the registrar's office maintains and monitors their academic progress. The function includes publishing course schedules, registering students for courses, handling changes in schedules once classes are underway, issuing official transcripts and diplomas, and maintaining statistical data. **Nature of work:** Admissions staff have many short term contacts with prospective students and parents and help them match their needs and interests with the right institution, which may not even be the institution of employment of the admission officer. Registrars work with students through their records, and may see individual students to process their schedules and provide services. **Qualifications:** Director-level jobs require experience and a master's or doctoral degree in college student personnel or higher education administration. Admission officers may be bachelor's degree staff, often graduates of that institution, or may have master's degrees in counseling or college student personnel. Some positions require marketing experience. Registrars have a variety of degrees, but must demonstrate administrative and management skills and computer literacy. Beginning staff often travel, and remuneration includes a travel allowance or use of a college car. **Common job titles:** Assistant or Associate Director, Dean of Admission or Admission and Records,

Registrar, Director of Enrollment Management, Coordinator of School Relations, Transfer Admission Specialist, Admission Officer or Admission Counselor. (Average salaries: Director of Admission and Registration, $50,000; Registrar, $43,272; Enrollment Management Director, $60,151; Admissions Counselor: $23,156.)

Career Development, Experiential Learning, and Student Employment Services

Responsibilities: College career centers assist students in developing meaningful career and employment aspirations. Career services include helping students choose a career direction and academic major, coordinating experiential learning programs to help students explore careers and integrate classroom learning with work experience, and assisting students in locating and securing jobs. On some campuses, career services may be part of the counseling center; experiential learning programs and employment services, sometimes called "placement," may be located within academic colleges or departments. Career development functions include individual counseling about career choice, choice of major, or career change; individual assessment and occupational testing; maintaining an occupational and employment resource library; alumni and community mentor programs; working with academic departments to design career courses and programs; and career or life planning programs or courses. Experiential learning functions include individual career and employment counseling, developing internship or cooperative education opportunities, working with faculty to help students define learning objectives for internships or co-ops, and teaching classes or seminars to help students integrate work with classroom learning. Employment services include seeking employers to hire students or graduates; individual career and employment counseling; workshops on resume preparation, interviewing, networking, and other employment topics; coordination of job or career fairs; coordinating interviews on the campus for employers; job bulletins and resume referral services; developing programs or events with academic departments. **Nature of work:** Career services include individual, group, and computer work with students. Counseling sessions and records are considered confidential. Students seeking career or job assistance may have other issues to resolve, such as indecision or parental or family concerns, so referral may be made to counselors, psychologists, or mental health professionals. Work involves counseling, advising, teaching, planning programs and events, job development, administration of services often via technology, conducting surveys and publishing reports, and consultation with faculty, staff, and employers. **Qualifications:** Most positions require a master's degree in counseling, college student personnel or development, or higher education with an emphasis on career development. Directors often need a doctoral degree and extensive experience. On some campuses, staff may also hold faculty appointments in counseling, college student personnel, or education. **Common job titles:** Career Counselor, Student Employment Specialist, Internship Coordinator, Associate or Assistant Director of Career Development, Director of Cooperative Education, Director of Career Services, Associate or Assistant Dean of Placement. (Average salary: Director of Career Development and Placement, $38,940.)

Commuter Programs and Off-Campus Housing

Responsibilities: Commuter students live nearby the campus with their parents or in their own homes or apartments. On many campuses, commuter students comprise a majority of the student body. Staff who work in commuter programs and off-campus housing programs serve as commuter advocates, provide off-campus housing and roommate locator services, help with issues such as commuter parking, or provide shuttle bus services. They keep other campus offices aware of commuter student needs. **Nature of work:** Staff provide direct services to commuters and may work with commuter student advisors. **Qualifications:** Most positions require a master's degree in college student personnel or higher education administration and strong administration, management, and programming skills. Candidates must be aware of adult student issues. **Common job titles:** Director or Assistant Director of Commuter Programs, Commuter Student Advisor or Coordinator of Off-Campus Housing.

Counseling and Testing

Responsibilities: Counseling and testing services are usually located in a counseling center comprised of a director and a staff of counselors and or psychologists. Staff work with individuals and groups on such issues as academic success, self-esteem, relationships, test anxiety, stress, sexuality and sexual concerns, career development, depression, suicidal thoughts, substance abuse, or eating disorders. Services are usually remedial, developmental, and preventive. Staff provide outreach programming to students in settings, such as residence halls or student organizations, and are frequently consultants to faculty and other professional staff. Counselors aid students and campus staff with crises. Counselors may teach courses in human relations or learning and communication skills. Testing is used to provide additional information about the student in counseling or to help students applying for post-graduate education (for example, the Graduate Record Examination, Medical College Admissions Test, Law School Admissions Test.) Staff may also conduct research to help understand student development and the counseling process. **Nature of work:** Counselors work confidentially with individual students and small groups of students seeking assistance with normal developmental life issues or more complex forms of personality dysfunction. The director performs administrative and management functions and on the smaller campus may also counsel individual students. Students may be referred to psychiatrists in the campus health service or off-campus facilities, particularly if medication is needed. **Qualifications:** Staff commonly need a doctoral degree in counseling psychology, clinical psychology, guidance and counseling, or counseling. On some campuses, staff hold faculty appointments in counseling, counselor education, psychology, or college student development. Staff may need licensure in the state in which the college is located. Smaller colleges or community colleges may hire staff with master's degrees for the same functions. **Common job titles:** Director of Counseling, Staff Counselor, Staff Psychologist, Counselor, Counseling Psychologist, Clinical Psychologist, Training Director, or Psychometrist (specialist in testing). (Average salary of the Director is $44,436.)

Disability Support Services

Responsibilities: This function provides direct assistance to students with various disabilities and insures campus compliance with the *Americans with Disabilities Act*. Staff work with other campus offices to ensure an effective campus environment for students with disabilities. They coordinate such programs as interpreter and note taking services for the hearing impaired, readers for the blind, accessibility maps, advocacy for the physically challenged, and testing programs for identifying learning disabilities. Staff coordinate residence hall accommodations for those with hearing, sight, and mobility challenges; special parking and transportation systems; academic support; and generally serve in an advocacy role, helping the campus adapt to the needs of students, faculty, and staff with disabilities. Staff also work closely with state vocational rehabilitation services. **Nature of work:** Staff work individually with students to assess needs and maintain needed supports. **Qualifications:** Most positions require a master's degree, often in rehabilitation counseling. **Common job titles:** Director or Assistant Director of Disability Support Services, Learning Disability Specialist, Counselor, Rehabilitation Counselor, or Interpreter.

Financial Aid

Responsibilities: Many students need financial assistance to enroll or remain enrolled in college. Financial aid officers assist individual students and their families in receiving appropriate forms of aid. They work with such programs as federal work study, federal and state aid programs, loan programs, and scholarships and grants. They advise students on the types and requirements of their aid, help with personal financial planning and budgeting, maintain eligibility records, and sometimes coordinate student employment programs. **Nature of work:** Financial aid staff have extensive contact with students and families about forms, records, and employment, and work individually with students to resolve financial stresses. **Qualifications:** Financial aid administration is a complex specialty with many regulations and procedures. A master's in higher education administration or college student personnel is often required. Computer literacy and financial aid experience during graduate study are preferred. **Common job titles:** Director, Associate or Assistant Director of Financial Aid, Financial Aid Counselor or Advisor. (Average salary for the Director is $42,300.)

Health Services

Responsibilities: The primary role of a health service is the physical well being and care of students provided primarily by physicians, nurses, nurse practitioners, and physicians assistants. A growing number of campus health centers also employ psychiatrists, psychologists, social workers, and counselors to assist students, and sometimes faculty and staff, with personal, social, and behavioral issues and health conditions which affect individual well being. Functions include individual assessment and diagnosis, individual and small group therapy, health education workshops and educational programs, and outreach to campus units. Social workers or counselors in health services see students with less severe problems. **Nature of work:** Psychiatrists are licensed physicians and can prescribe medication to assist with acute or more severe problems. Issues may involve personality disorders, chronic depression, suicidal thoughts, substance abuse, eating disorders, paranoia, sexual dysfunction, as well as prolonged stress or anxiety, mild depression, relationship, or family problems. Mental health professionals may also provide individual counseling to students; facilitate support groups or direct programs for victims of date or acquaintance rape, those suffering from AIDS or other critical illnesses; and conduct educational programs to encourage safe and responsible sexual relations, and to prevent alcohol and substance abuse. **Qualifications:** A medical degree plus extensive training in psychiatry are required to be a licensed psychiatrist. Psychologists generally have a counseling or clinical psychology doctorate and are licensed according to state regulations. Others may have a master's degree in social work, counseling, or a related area. Some opportunities may exist for individuals with bachelor's degrees and specialized training in substance abuse. **Common job titles:** Physician, Psychiatrist, Psychologist, Staff Counselor, Health Educator, Nurse, Nurse Practitioner, Physician's Assistant, Director of Mental Health Services, Director or Assistant Director of Health Education. (Average salary for Physician director of student health services, $83,600; Nurse director of student health services, $31,404.)

Human Resources, Human Relations, and Employee Assistance

Responsibilities: Helping professionals can be employed by campus personnel or human resources offices. Some campuses include human relations programs (affirmative action compliance, sexual harassment, intergroup conflict mediation) in the human resources office, others have a separate human relations office. Some offices provide employment and career counseling, others conduct employee assistance programs, still others design and conduct staff training and development programs. **Nature of work:** Staff in human relations or resources work primarily with faculty and staff. They may interview applicants, assess their capabilities, and administer tests for campus employment; assist faculty or staff whose employment has been terminated and may counsel faculty and staff in choosing or changing careers and jobs. Staff trainers design and conduct skill building workshops and short courses in topics such as stress management, dealing with difficult people, successful job search tactics, understanding the campus financial system, supervision skills, or computer skills. Employee assistance programs provide individual and group assistance for faculty and staff with addictions and alcohol or substance abuse problems, as well as family, personal or on-the-job problems that are inhibiting work performance. **Common job titles:** Manager, Director, or Assistant Director of Human Resources, Human Relations, or Personnel; Personnel Representative; Human Relations or Human Resources Specialist; Affirmative Action Officer; Campus Compliance Officer; Training and Development Coordinator; or Employee Assistance Coordinator.

Leadership and Community Service

Responsibilities: Leadership programs may be offered for student leaders who hold various campus roles like sorority presidents, resident assistants, or student government officers. Leadership programs, workshops, institutes, and courses also are available to students who seek to develop their own leadership skills, but do not hold leadership positions. Leadership frequently is combined with community service. Community service involves identifying sites on and off campus for service involvement, training and supervising students who engage in service, and reflecting or processing the experience with the students. **Nature of work:** Staff design learning activities to help students develop leadership skills and community service orientations. Some may teach courses in leadership or service learning. Staff counsel, supervise, and help students process learning on and off site. **Qualifications:** Staff usually have a master's degree in counseling, college student personnel, or higher education administration. **Common job titles:** Director or Assistant Director of Student Activities for Leadership, Director of Community Service.

Orientation and Entry Services

Responsibilities: Staff in these offices aid new students in their adjustment to campus life. They work primarily with first-year students and transfer students when they first enroll. They design and coordinate new student orientation sessions, including placement testing to determine appropriate course levels, provide discussions of campus life, and course advising; teach orientation courses; conduct parent and family programs; and host parent or family weekends. **Nature of work:** Orientation staff supervise upper class orientation leaders and work with new students individually and in groups. Staff may teach freshman experience courses. **Qualifications:** Master's degree in counseling, college student personnel, or higher education administration is required with work experience in new student issues. **Common job titles:** Dean, Director, or Assistant Director of Orientation, Dean of Freshmen, Coordinator of Freshmen Experience.

Residence Life and Housing

Responsibilities: Residence life staff are specialists in group living, peer interaction, and community building. Staff are concerned with educational and social programming, roommate compatibility, floor standards, discipline, crisis management, and individual and group development. Entry level staff supervise undergraduate student staff (often called resident assistants or RAs), desk workers, custodial, and security staff. Residence halls may be single sex, coeducational, living-learning centers, or special interest housing, such as language houses, family housing, graduate housing, apartment housing, fraternities or sororities, international student housing, off-campus housing for commuters, or faculty housing. These offices often manage a summer conference program to use residence facilities on a year round basis. Hall sizes range from 50 to over 1,000 residents per building. Entry level staff usually live in their residence halls. Residence life programs are usually the largest employer of student affairs professionals. **Nature of work:** Entry staff work with students in a live-in, 24-hour-per-day situation. They plan educational programs around complex needs, such as adjustment to college, discipline, crisis intervention, conflict resolution, and personal advising. Assistant directors work with staff selection, training, and development. **Qualifications:** Most positions require a master's degree in counseling, college student personnel, or higher education administration. Some campuses have graduate and undergraduate students living in residence as resident assistants, and hire professionals with a master's degree as the area directors who supervise them. Positions that are live-in usually include salary plus apartment, utilities, and food plan. **Common job titles:** Director of Housing and Residence Life, Area Coordinator, Community Director, Hall Director, Head Resident, Training Director, Area Manager, Facilities Director and Business Manager. (Average salaries: Director of Student Housing, $38,837; Housing officer, residence life: $28,000.)

Services for Special Student Populations

Responsibilities: Various multicultural, gender, ethnic, or racial groups often benefit from special services designed to form community and meet special needs. Such programs include African-American, Asian, Hispanic, and Native American student groups; student centers; or international student offices. Other programs might include women's centers or gay, lesbian, or bisexual student organizations. Staff working with these programs advise students individually, plan topical programs, serve as advocates for these students on campus, educate campus staff and faculty about students' special needs, and provide support programs. Small colleges may not have separate centers for all special groups, while large universities may have separate programs. **Nature of work:** Staff interact socially and academically with individual students and groups of students. The office or center frequently becomes home base and students drop by regularly, providing both informal and formal contact. **Qualifications:** Most positions require a master's degree in counseling or college student personnel, or from another major, such as African-American studies, women's studies, or international education. On some campuses, staff may hold a joint appointment with an academic department. Frequently staff are members of the special group with whom they are working (for example, a women's center usually has women staff). **Common job titles:** Director or Assistant Director of the Center, Black Student Advisor, Director of Multicultural or Minority Programs, International Student Advisor. (Average salaries: Director of Minority Affairs, $40,000; Director of International Students, $34,500.)

Student Activities and Student Programming

Responsibilities: Student activities involve a wide range of programs, including student organizations, student union programming, and intramural or recreational sports programs. Staff in student activities advise various student organizations; schedule non-academic campus space; advise student government; work with student media, such as campus radio or newspapers; publish the student handbook or yearbook; develop, enforce and interpret campus rules and regulations; and develop and implement a broad range of campus cultural, social, and educational programming. This office is challenged to meet the diverse interests of many campus groups. The student union is the "living room" of the campus: usually a centrally located building with many services, such as the bookstore, lounges, meeting rooms, movie theater, bowling lanes, ballroom, cafeterias and restaurants, branch bank, student government offices, and student affairs offices. Professional staff schedule space; raise money; plan programs, such as film festivals, cultural festivals, recreation and tournaments, topical forums; and advise student groups. Intramural or recreation programs include club sports; campus competitions between student organizations, such as fraternities and sororities or residence halls; and faculty and staff leagues. Recreation programs frequently include intramural programs, but also include outing clubs, tournaments, and games. Recreation staff occasionally report to intercollegiate athletics. On small campuses, recreation and intramural programs may be part of student activities. **Nature of work:** Staff work closely with student leaders and with students in groups and organizations. Work is fast paced with many students regularly in and out of a bustling office. Large student unions may have over 20,000 student visits per day. **Qualifications:** Entry positions require a master's degree in college student development, or higher education administration. In addition, these positions may require experience in the entertainment or fine arts areas. Counseling degrees are also acceptable with administrative skill and experience. Many of the recreation or sports positions require physical education or recreation degrees or direct athletic experiences. **Common job titles:** Dean, Director, Associate or Assistant Dean of Student Activities, Director of Campus Activities, Student Activity Advisor or Counselor, Director of Greek Life, Panhellenic or Intrafraternity Council Advisor. (Average salary: Director of Student Activities, $32,755.) Director, Associate or Assistant Director of the Student Union or Campus Union, Programming Coordinator or Advisor. (Average salary: Director of Student Union, $42,924.) Director of Intramurals or Recreation or Recreation Aide. (Average Salary: Director, Campus Recreation and Intramural, $35,930.)

PROFESSIONAL INVOLVEMENT AND SUPPORT

When you take a position in student affairs, there are many professional associations and opportunities for involvement. In addition to the American Counseling Association (ACA), numerous general professional societies, such as the American College Personnel Association (ACPA), the National Association of Student Personnel Administrators (NASPA) or the National Association of Women in Education (NAWE), and specialty associations, such as the American College and University Housing Officers International (ACUHO-I), the National Association of Campus Activities (NACA), National Career Development Association (NCDA), the American Psychological Association (APA), or the National Orientation Directors Association (NODA) provide special journals, ethical standards, professional development activities, and leadership opportunities. Professionals have opportunities to meet on campus, in the region, or at national or international conventions to share new programs, research findings, and improved approaches to common problems. When faced with a perplexing problem at work, staff telephone or e-mail professional colleagues who are always ready to help! Student affairs professionals work in a collaborative, sharing, and supportive field.

For more information on careers in student affairs work requiring counseling and human development credentials, talk with a student affairs professional at a college near you, attend a program sponsored at a nearby college during "National Careers in Student Affairs Week" (usually the last week in October), attend a conference in the state or region (see listings in the *Chronicle of Higher Education*), or read the following publications in "Recommended Readings."

ADDITIONAL INFORMATION AND RESOURCES

Associations (See Appendix A for addresses)

American Counseling Association
American College Counseling Association
American College Personnel Association
American College Unions International
American Psychological Association
Association of College and University Housing Officers
    International
Association of Fraternity Advisors
Cooperative Education Association
National Association for Campus Activities
National Association for Women in Education
National Association of Colleges and Employers
National Association of Student Employment Administrators
National Association of Student Personnel Administrators
National Career Development Association
National Clearinghouse for Commuter Programs
National Intramural and Recreational Sports Association
National Orientation Directors Association
National Society for Experiential Education

The following books and articles contain additional information:

Baxter, N. J. (1994). *Opportunities in counseling and development careers.* Chicago, IL: VGM Career Horizons, NTC Publishing Group. (Describes functions of counselor in variety of settings, including college; chapters on educational programs, licensure, and future trends and issues.)

CAS standards and guidelines for student services/development programs. C/O Vice President for Student Affairs, the University of Maryland, College Park, 20742. (Contains standards for graduate preparation programs and for most Student Affairs functional areas.)

Garner, G. O. (1994). *Careers in Social and Rehabilitation Services.* Chicago, IL:VGM Career Horizons, NTC Publishing Group. (Includes chapter on educational services including college student affairs professionals.)

Komives, S. R., Woodard, D. & Assoc. (anticipated 1996). *Student services: A handbook for the profession.* (3rd ed.) San Francisco, CA: Jossey-Bass. (A textbook used in many first year master's degree programs.)

Kiem, M.B. & Grahman, J (Eds). (1994). *A directory of graduate preparation programs in college student personnel.* A publication of the American College Personnel Association--Commission XII: Graduate Preparation Programs. Washington, D.C. : American College Personnel Association (Contains graduate entrance requirements, master's and doctoral curriculum and information about graduate faculty of over 100 graduate programs.)

Kirby, A.F., & Woodard, D. (Eds). (1983). *Career perspectives in student affairs.* NASPA Monograph Series, Vol. 1. Washington, D.C.: National Association of Student Personnel Administrators. (Contains chapters for new professionals, women, and career advancement issues.)

Rentz, A. L., & Saddlemire, G. L. (Eds). (1988). *Student affairs functions in higher education.* Springfield, IL: Charles C. Thomas. (Describes the work in many functional areas and career paths in Student Affairs.)

Chapter 5

CAREERS IN BUSINESS AND INDUSTRY

Bree Hayes
Pamela O. Paisley

People typically imagine counselors or other helping professionals at work in settings like schools, mental health centers, hospitals, or private practices. Many people believe that counselors primarily help people who are having problems. These are not the only settings where counselors work. For example, in recent years, both small businesses and major corporations have come to realize that in running an effective business, their most valuable resources are their employees. Additionally, the labor market has undergone significant changes in terms of workers and the type of work performed. In response to these factors, programs that address employees' needs for personal and professional development have proliferated--there has been an increased demand for people with counseling skills to work in business and industry. Counselors in these settings do not always fill the traditional role of counseling people about their personal problems; instead, they often combine counseling and consultation skills with specialized business knowledge. This chapter addresses the diverse roles and responsibilities of counselors in business and industry.

THE BEGINNING OF A NEW ERA

As World War II ended, 50 years ago, weary soldiers returned to the families and jobs they had left behind, bringing with them a serious problem. The stress of war had left its mark on some of these veterans in the form of alcoholism or problem drinking. Many of these veterans were returning to jobs in plants and factories where the use of heavy equipment was a routine part of their work. Try to imagine an inebriated worker moving large tractors or working with dangerous machinery, such as an acetylene welder, and you can begin to see the problem. These workers were not only endangering their own lives, but also the lives of their coworkers; and, if they were able to make it through the day without an accident, they were not very productive. Quickly, it became clear that something had to be done to decrease accidents and increase productivity. Companies all over America began to establish programs to assist employees with drinking problems.

EMPLOYEE ASSISTANCE PROGRAMS

Employee assistance programs (EAPs) offer many services to businesses and employees. The scope of EAP services has expanded to include marriage and family problems, financial concerns, alcohol and other drug-related problems, legal concerns, and any other human problems or questions that might affect an employee's job performance.

Within the EAP field, there are two clearly defined jobs for counselors. First, there is the job of the EAP counselor and, second, there is the job of the EAP administrator. EAP counselors are available to assess employee problems or answer questions. EAP administrators oversee the program in its entirety.

EAP counselors meet with employees in a confidential setting to determine the nature of their concerns. Relationships between EAP counselors and employees are usually short-term and focus on problem assessment and referral to appropriate community resources. Referrals are made to a wide spectrum of community agencies, including mental health centers, alcohol treatment centers, and credit counseling services, as well as to private practitioners such as attorneys, counselors, and psychologists.

It is important for EAP counselors to be current in their knowledge of referral resources. They must understand the services different agencies provide, the costs that are involved, and the expertise of the professionals who deliver these services. The EAP counselor provides all this information to the employee in the counseling or assessment session. After the EAP counselor and employee have considered available resources, the counselor helps the employee contact the appropriate community resource. In sum, EAP counselors are professionals trained to listen to people's concerns, to assess the extent of their problems, and to assist them in getting the help they need to alleviate or cope with their problems.

In the past, EAP counselors were not trained professionally, but instead were often recovering alcoholics (Dickman, Challenger, Emener, & Hutchison, 1988). Although they had no formal training, they were well experienced with alcoholism and, therefore, could be very helpful to people who were struggling with this particular problem. Today, EAP counselors are professionally trained--usually holding a master's degree in counseling, social work, or psychology. To become a Certified Employee Assistance Professional (CEAP), one must have EAP experience and pass a written examination. It should also be noted that while the original Employee Assistance Programs emerged in response to substance abuse concerns, today's EAP counselors deal with a range of issues. Pre-service and in-service training requirements are rigorous, but the rewards can be many. Most EAP counselors report that their work is challenging, highly variable, and offers adequate to comfortable financial rewards, with a beginning salary range of $27,500-$38,500.

EAP Administrators

The role of the EAP administrator is to coordinate the overall delivery of EAP services. This effort incorporates a wide range of responsibilities, beginning with program design. Each company's EAP is unique. It is imperative that EAPs match the specific needs of the organizations they serve, so EAP administrators spend time with a company's personnel or human services department to establish consistent policies and procedures for use of the EAP. Next, the EAP administrator conducts training sessions for employees and supervisors to describe the program and answer questions.

The EAP administrator monitors and evaluates programs. EAP administrators prepare reports for companies to determine an EAP's use effectiveness. They must also plan and carry out changes to enhance programs if reports indicate ineffectiveness.

Another on-going task of the EAP administrator is to distribute program marketing materials to employees and supervisors. Effective EAPs are highly visible and are used frequently. Their degree of effectiveness is achieved through the dissemination of pamphlets, posters, and articles in company newspapers. All of these tasks fall under the responsibility of the EAP administrator. Finally, an EAP administrator is on call at all times to ensure that an EAP counselor is available to attend to any program problems, and to serve as a liaison to company officials.

The work of EAP administrators is demanding, ever changing, and requires great attention to detail. Whether the employing organization is large or small, the demands are the same. Typically EAP administrators are well experienced, attentive to details, have outgoing personalities, and do not mind erratic work schedules. Many hold graduate degrees, including doctorates, in counseling, social work, or psychology. They have generally earned their CEAP. Beginning salaries for EAP administrators range from $38,500-$55,000.

CAREER COUNSELING

The vocational guidance movement emerged at the beginning of the 20th century as a result of numerous political, economic, and educational factors within American society. Examples of these factors include social reform efforts following the Industrial Revolution, interest in the study and measurement of individual differences, federal legislation, and the very significant contributions of early pioneers in this field, such as Frank Parsons and Jesse B. Davis. Originally, career or vocational guidance was focused on initial career choice with emphasis on a systematic decision-making process. Over the years, vocational choice and career development has been reconceptualized as a life-span and developmental process, having implications for people at all stages and ages of development and addressing a wide range of career-related issues and situations.

Career Counselors

Career counselors in business and industry settings are a relatively new phenomenon. Their appearance in this setting may be directly correlated with a changing work force, new technology, and changes in society's attitude about quality of work life. For the past decade, major corporations have found that they must attend to employee professional development on many levels. A critical demand has arisen to assist all employees in determining which job best fits their personal and professional needs.

Second, new technology has improved efficiency, but, in many cases, it has displaced employees from their jobs. Assembly-line workers who once routinely attached parts to pieces of machinery are being replaced by robots. Keypunch operators are being replaced by computers. Receptionists are being replaced by electronic telephone answering machines. Delivery persons are being replaced by electronic mail. Employees who perform these tasks are good workers who provide important services and would like to continue to work, but where can they go in the organization if they are displaced by new technology?

Finally, the work ethic in America is changing. In the past, major corporations frequently asked their employees to pull up stakes and move on a regular basis. This practice might result in as many as 10 or 12 moves over the employee's life with the company. Until recently, nearly one in every five American families moved each year. The trend is for employees to be far less willing to relocate for their employer's convenience. They prefer to find other positions within the company that allow them to remain in their current location. Workers also seem more sensitive to finding a balance between work and family. Unlike the generations of workers that preceded them, they do not view work as the primary focus of their lives. Many employees adjust their careers within the organization to find a position that provides balance.

To help them in making such decisions, employees are using the services of career counselors. Corporations hire counselors to assist their employees in these efforts. In other cases, companies use the services of outside consultants. Career counselors work with employees to assess their skills, abilities, and interests and to explore career opportunities that fit these variables. Counselors obtain information from employees through interviews, tests, and employee self-exploration. The final decision about choice of career remains with the employee.

Career counselors generally hold a master's or a higher degree in counseling, social work, or psychology and have specialized training in career development. Many career counselors are certified as National Certified Career Counselors (NCCC) [see Chapter 11]. To obtain this certification, one must have considerable experience and take a comprehensive written examination.

Beginning salaries are highly variable and seem to be directly influenced by whether the counselor is a full-time employee or an outside consultant. Career counselors working for a specific corporation might begin at a salary of $25,300- $33,800 depending on education and experience. Outside consultants, who typically charge as much as $100 per hour, could make considerably more money, depending on the number of hours spent in consulting.

Outplacement Counselors

Another specialty within the field of career counseling in business and industry is outplacement counseling. When employees are terminated, or entire plants or offices are closed, companies recognize that employees may need outplacement assistance because they may have limited job-seeking skills. Through training and personal counseling sessions, outplacement counselors give employees the skills they need to develop resumes, interview with confidence, and obtain new positions. Outplacement counselors have the same training as other career counselors, with a specialty in outplacement services. Their income is highly variable because it is determined by calculating a percentage of the salaries of the terminated employees, perhaps with bonuses for each terminated employee who is placed in a new position. As with other career counseling, these services may be provided as an in-house or contracted program.

HUMAN RESOURCES

Critical to the daily functioning of any organization is its human resources department. Members of this department are generally concerned with the overall recruitment, development, management, and effectiveness of an organization's person power. The jobs within the field of human resources are highly variable and offer many employment possibilities to individuals who have had training in business, management, or many of the helping professions. In most small companies one person is responsible for the entire human resources operation. In larger companies the human resources department may include as many as 20 different job titles. What follows is a description of the major positions within the human resources field.

Human Resources Managers

The title of human resources manager is a relatively new one and replaces the old title of personnel manager. The primary function of a human resources manager is to oversee all programs and policies related to employees. Specific tasks include implementing established personnel policies; formulating and recommending new policies; overseeing employee recruitment, placement, and training; administering wage and salary policies; overseeing all labor-management functions; supervising disbursement of benefits and compensation; and, generally overseeing all of the human resource functions that have been previously described in this chapter.

These professionals are highly experienced and generally hold bachelor's or master's degrees in business, management, counseling, psychology, or social work. Their salaries range from $55,800 - $132,000 depending on the size of the company and the scope of their responsibilities. Their jobs are challenging and demanding and, therefore, require patience, tact, high energy, and creativity.

Employment Recruiters

Employment recruiters seek prospective employees and develop the means to attract them to their organizations. For example, if a company needs to hire new engineers, its employment recruiters will establish relationships with university engineering departments. Employment recruiters also establish close working relationships with human resources specialists in similar companies or related fields. Other responsibilities include the advertising of positions in professional or trade journals and newspapers, interaction with search firms and employment agencies, and the general release of information about job availability. An employment recruiter must arrange meetings with prospective candidates on an individual or group basis. During these meetings, recruiters describe jobs more thoroughly than they might in a journal ad and attempt to encourage candidates to meet with the company's employment interviewer.

Employment recruiters typically hold bachelor's degrees in business, management, psychology, or social work. Because it is frequently an entry-level position, this job requires little previous experience. It does, however, require high energy, an outgoing personality, and a willingness to travel. Beginning salaries range from $22,000 - $27,500.

Employment Interviewers

Employment interviewers serve a vital role in the human resources department. Their first job is to discuss specific requirements for job vacancies with appropriate management personnel. Based on these discussions, they conduct screening interviews with prospective employees to determine whether a candidate's qualifications match the company's needs. The interview process also includes verifying a candidate's employment history, educational background, and references.

Employment interviewers typically make job offers to successful candidates and may negotiate salaries. They frequently conduct new employee orientation. They may also conduct exit interviews with employees who are leaving the company.

Educational preparation for this position usually includes a bachelor's degree in business, management, psychology, or social work. Interviewers generally have had some experience in other human resources areas before undertaking this position. It is helpful if the interviewer is warm and personable, attentive to detail, and does not mind working long hours during periods of corporate expansion or reduction. Beginning salaries range from $27,500 - $38,500.

Employee Services Managers

Employee services managers establish, administer, and coordinate company-sponsored employee services. Specific tasks of this effort include coordinating the service awards program; arranging company-sponsored social activities; disseminating information and publications of interest to employees; assisting employees with relocation; participating in credit union activities; and supervising all employee recreation activities, including physical fitness and wellness programs.

This entry-level position is generally found only in large companies. Formal training requires a bachelor's degree in recreation, psychology, social work, or management. It is very important that individuals in this position have outgoing, positive personalities and are willing to work with many kinds of people in a variety of situations. Beginning salaries range from $19,800 - $25,300.

Equal Employment Opportunity Managers

Equal Employment Opportunity (EEO) managers establish and implement corporate affirmative action/equal employment opportunity programs. Their primary concern is that employees and potential employees be treated fairly and in compliance with government legislation and management's directives regardless of sex, age, race, ability, or veteran's status.

Specifically, EEO managers' responsibilities include establishing and monitoring EEO affirmative action programs for all segments of the company; reviewing company practices related to the hiring, training, transfer, and promotion of minority and female employees; analyzing job content to ensure that job titles and compensation are commensurate with work performed; investigating discrimination charges; developing a list from which female and minority candidates may be selected when jobs arise; ensuring that all tests used for hiring, promotion, or transfer have been evaluated professionally to eliminate bias; and keeping management apprised of changing governmental requirements.

Training for this position is highly variable. Some companies employ the services of attorneys as EEO managers; others use human resources specialists who may hold a bachelor's degree in business, management, psychology, or social work. EEO managers must have current knowledge of government legislation and company policy. EEO managers must be assertive and comfortable with confrontation, because a routine part of their job is to address company errors. The salary for EEO specialists ranges from $35,000-$50,000.

Training Specialists

Training specialists are primarily concerned with the professional development of employees. Specific tasks include analyzing employee training needs, designing training programs, developing training manuals, purchasing and maintaining training equipment, and conducting training sessions. This role for counselors within business and industry is becoming increasingly significant.

Professionals in this field may work exclusively for the company in its training department, or be employed as outside consultants. Frequently, even companies that have "in-house" trainers hire outside trainers if they need a particular area of expertise to solve a given problem. In either case, training specialists are well educated and hold a doctoral or master's degree in business, management, counseling, psychology, or social work. Many trainers have had additional preparation in public speaking and effective communication. Salaries vary widely. Trainers who work only for one company usually receive a fixed salary, whereas outside trainers charge by the hour, day, or project. Training specialists must be current in their information, comfortable making presentations to groups of nearly any size, creative, and charismatic.

Counselors as trainers in business and industry are becoming increasingly significant due to the variety of programs needed. Diversity training, stress reduction, interpersonal communication, and team-building are examples of the types of topics identified by business as training needs for which counselors are particularly effective providers.

Organizational Consultants

Organizational consultants assess problems or concerns of a particular company and assist in resolving these issues. Examples of the type of concerns these consultants address include poor employee morale, low productivity, poor customer relations, or high employee turnover. They also assist in preparing for layoffs, downsizing, or expansion. Organizational consultants typically follow a three-step procedure. First, they assess the problem, which is generally accomplished by interviewing key personnel. Second, they make suggestions to management, both verbally and as a part of a written report. Third, they assist in implementing the changes by helping to create new policies, conducting training, or working with individual employees.

Unlike the jobs that were described previously, organizational consultants rarely work directly for the company that uses their services. Their work requires an ability to step back from the organization and see it without preconceived ideas. This is best done by someone who has no internal ties or personal relationships with the company's employees; therefore, external organizational consultants usually are employed on a short-term contract for one specific task rather than to be a full-time employee of the company they are serving.

Organizational consultants are highly specialized and well trained. They often hold advanced graduate degrees in business, management, counseling, psychology, or social work. They have spent time working with companies in various capacities. Successful consultants are knowledgeable, competent, articulate, natural leaders, and tactful. This last trait is of particular importance, because the very nature of their work requires them to tell a company how to improve the way it is operating. Many corporations are implementing Total Quality Management (TQM) or empowerment models that require different and enhanced managerial skills. The organizational consultant often serves as coach or counselor to the chief executive (Smith, 1993).

Organizational consultants charge by the hour, day, or project. Beginning salaries are variable, but consultants can earn from $55,000 - $99,000.

A GROWING NEED

As American factories and offices recognize the need for more humane work environments, the need for counselors, psychologists, and social workers will continue to grow. In some ways, these helping professionals are like all other helping professionals. In other ways, they are quite unique. The basic counseling skills are essential; however, more specialized skills in consultation and business related issues are also necessary. A career in business and industry is not right for everyone, but for those who would find this work challenging, the door is wide open.

ADDITIONAL INFORMATION AND RESOURCES

You can find additional information about careers in business and industry from your counselor or career center. You might want to read those sections of the *Occupational Outlook Handbook* (OOH) that describe occupations mentioned in this chapter. The book by Lewis and Lewis (1986), listed in the References gives a good description of occupational skills and choices. The *Business Index* is also helpful in locating relevant articles to identify trends, needs, and opportunities.

Professional associations mentioned in this chapter are listed in the Appendix with addresses so you can write for further information.

The following books and articles provide additional information on this topic:

Dickman, F., Challenger, B.R., Emener, W.G., & Hutchison, W.S., Jr. (1988). *Employee assistance programs: A basic text.* Springfield, IL: Charles C Thomas.

Lewis, J.A., & Lewis, M.D. (1986). *Counseling programs for employees in the workplace.* Monterey, CA: Brooks/Cole.

Smith, L. (1993, December). The executive's new coach. *Fortune, 128* (16), 126.

U.S. Department of Labor. (1994). *Occupational outlook handbook* (1994- 1995 ed.). Washington, DC: Author.

Wegmann, R., Chapman, R., & Johnson, M. (1989). *Work in the new economy: Careers and job seeking into the 21st century* (Revised ed.). Indianapolis, IN: JIST Works, Inc.

Chapter 6

CAREERS IN PRIVATE PRACTICE

Burt Bertram

Private practice is completely different than any other setting discussed in this book. So different, in fact, that a specific description of the typical private practice almost defies definition. Across the country, privately practicing mental health practitioners have established thousands of different practice configurations. Each of these "practices" reflects a unique combination of services based upon the business skills and professional competencies of the practitioner.

In the simplest terms, private practice involves the selling of the practitioner's professional skills in the open marketplace. To remain in business, private practitioners must satisfy their customers (clients). In many ways, private practice often has as much in common with owning and operating a restaurant or auto garage as it does with the practice of counseling as experienced in an institutional setting. Success in private practice is ultimately based on retaining existing clients and referral sources and identifying and capitalizing on new market opportunities.

Before venturing too far into an attempt to describe the activities of a private practitioner, an important disclaimer must be offered. Most mental health private practitioners are involved, to a greater or lesser extent, in delivering services through the current patchwork health care system of America--a system in the midst of profound change. Cost containment pressures, at every level, are forcing a complete reconfiguration of the delivery of mental health services. Every day the playing field is different. What is true one day is just a blip on the screen of the trajectory of change; therefore, it is impossible to predict what the future of private practice will look like. Suffice to say, people will continue to need counseling and psychotherapy services; the issue is, how will the private practice mental health professional fit into the new service delivery paradigm?

Four key variables associated with private practice will likely remain regardless of whatever changes are brought by health care reform. The four variables are (a) the practice business structure, (b) the clinical or client specialty, (c) additional services, and (d) payment sources.

PRIVATE PRACTICE VARIABLES

Practice Business Structure

Private practice business structures run the gamut from the very simple to the very complex.   There are advantages and disadvantages to each.

Solo Practice involves only one mental health professional who may, or may not, employ clerical or reception staff. Simplicity is the primary advantage of this type of structure as the practitioner can make decisions without negotiating with affiliates or partners. Professional isolation and full responsibility for all overhead expenses are the primary disadvantages. Clinically, the solo practitioner faces additional difficulties in finding other professionals for case consultation and supervision.

Rent Sharing Affiliation is characterized by a loose confederation structure, usually built around shared office rent and other common expenses including clerical assistance. Historically this arrangement has probably been the most popular business structure for private practitioners.   The advantages are obvious; the disadvantages are buried in the particulars of the relationships among the affiliates. Costs are lower because several practitioners share overhead expenses. The arrangement reduces professional and social isolation by providing built-in opportunities for workplace friendships and clinical collaboration and consultation.

Instability and potential professional liability exposure are the primary disadvantages. Affiliates often "come and go" from these loose rent sharing structures with little sense of group identity. This transient nature can create a sense of professional detachment within these loosely defined groups. Additionally, professional affiliation often mistakenly communicates a corporate or group structure message to clients that can result in each affiliate being legally held for the actual or alleged unprofessional conduct of all other affiliates.

Group Practice occurs in many forms and can involve members/partners from one discipline--e.g., mental health counseling, or can be multi-disciplinary involving members from several different mental health disciplines--e.g., psychiatry, psychology, social work, marriage and family therapy, or counseling. The group practice usually employs a staff of support personnel and, when successful, often employs other mental health professionals. The advantages, both financial and clinical, of a formal group partnership or professional corporation are many. The potential complications and disadvantages are also just as numerous. A group structure provides opportunities for cost sharing, cross referral, and contracting with managed care and other purchasers of services. Additionally, different clinical perspectives, resulting from different training and orientation among the members, can provide rich opportunities for collaborative care of clients. The long-term financial advantages associated with a successful group practice, as compared with the other practice structures, can not be over estimated; however, in addition to these potential advantages are all the disadvantages that come with complexity, diversity, and size. Financial start-up costs and monthly expenses are significantly higher with this arrangement and there is no escaping the shared liability implications.

Clinical/Client Speciality

While a general counseling practice is possible, most practitioners focus on particular client issues or client populations. The determination of a speciality is driven by the interests and background of the practitioner as well as the areas of expertise that the practitioner has developed. A complete listing of all speciality areas would be impossible as they represent every conceivable life span issue or circumstance and every demographic group. A representative sample of life span counseling issues includes bereavement, divorce, parent-child, pain management, chronic illness, drug/alcohol abuse, marital conflict, post traumatic stress disorder, co-dependency, panic disorders, anxiety, sexual dysfunction, childhood physical/sex abuse, infertility, school adjustment, empty nest and mid-life crisis, and hundreds of others. Demographically defined specialities could include children, adolescents, young adults, mid-life adults, older adults, African-Americans, Hispanics, Asians, Jews, Catholics,

Lutherans, Agnostics, Gays, Bi-racial couples, adoptions, re-marriage and blended families and hundreds of other demographically defined groups.

Practitioners often choose certain demographic groups and then develop specialities based on the treatment of life span issues or medically necessary diagnoses. Ultimately, these decisions are driven by the availability of clients, competitive marketplace factors, and the availability of resources for the purchase of these services.

Additional Services

While most of our attention has been directed toward "counseling" as the mental health service, it is important to note that private practitioners often develop expertise in a variety of additional services other than counseling and psychotherapy. These additional services are only restricted by the resourcefulness, creativity, and marketing energy of the practitioner. A sampling of additional services includes marital/domestic mediation, parent education, workplace team building, stress management/biofeedback, public education seminars and workshops, colleague training and supervision, home study evaluations for adoptions and custody, and professional writing.

Sources of Income

The final variable associated with the establishment of a successful private practice addresses three questions: Who will pay for the services? How will the payment be made? How much will be paid for the services? Accurately answering these questions is essential to establishing and maintaining long term success in private practice.

In most cases, payment for services occurs in three general ways: (a) Payment directly from the client receiving the service; (b) Payment indirectly through the client's insurance or managed care company; and (c) Payment through a contract for purchase of services by a school, community agency, or other group/organization.

The four variables discussed above are inter-related and interactive. The over-riding business questions are: What opportunities exist? What services will be purchased by the consumer that are consistent with the practitioner's professional interest and expertise? The answer to these inter-related questions will be driven by a careful analysis of the needs of the service area to include the client population's ability and willingness to pay for the specialities and services offered by the practitioner. Marketplace competition or saturation--e.g., how many providers are available to the potential client-- must also be considered. Once these issues are determined, the structure of the practice should be designed to fulfill the realization of the opportunities.

INCOME OPPORTUNITIES FOR PRIVATE PRACTITIONERS

Income in private practice is based on market conditions and the practitioner's ability to competently attend to both the delivery of quality mental health services and the demands of small business management. *Psychotherapy Finances,* a monthly newsletter, provides guidance to mental health practitioners regarding the management of their practice and their money. They publish annual results of fee and income surveys of the subscribers to their publication. Survey results published in January, 1995, provide a snapshot of private practice income from the more than 1,700 practitioner respondents. Median fees (usual and customary) reported for a 50 minute counseling hour were as follows: marriage/family therapist $80, professional counselors $80, social workers $80, psychologists $95, and psychiatrists $120. These are median (most frequent) fees. The fees charged by professional counselors and marriage/family therapists ranged from under $50 to over $100 per hour depending upon a host of variables including experience of the practitioner, practice location, financial ability of clients, specialized expertise of the clinician, and contracts with managed care and other volume discounts for group purchase of services.

Results from the survey indicated annual net income (after operating expenses, before taxes) for professional counselors ranged from over $25,000 to $100,000 with a median (most frequent) income of $45,200. For marriage/family therapists, the range of net income was similar while the median income was $46,300. Psychologists, on the other hand, report a similar range but the median income of $75,000 far exceeds professional counselors and marriage/family therapists.

PERSONAL CHARACTERISTICS OF PRIVATE PRACTITIONERS

Successful private practitioners must possess special characteristics related to the development and management of a small business. These business-person characteristics begin with the acceptance that success or failure rests squarely on your shoulders. Everything that occurs or fails to occur in the practice is your responsibility. As with all things, there is a tension between the exhilaration of being your own boss and the 24-hour, seven-day-per-week reality of knowing that you are responsible for your success. Successful private practitioners must be self-starters. They must be people who can define for themselves what needs to be done and then do it themselves, or see to it that it is accomplished by someone else.

Private practice, like any business, is either growing or declining. Private practitioners must be willing and able to constantly market their practice by seeking out new opportunities for community visibility, contacting new referral sources, and maintaining effective working relationships with existing referral sources. The ability and willingness to sell yourself as competent and caring is critical to private practice success.

In private practice, money is always an issue. Practitioners must be able to decide what their time is worth, based on their experience, education, and the norms of the community. Can the practitioner securely and professionally state a fee and then assertively, without apology, collect the fee? Can the practitioner negotiate with managed care and other purchasers of services regarding services and fees?

Managing the business side of the practice includes setting-up and maintaining an office space, keeping up with billing, paying the bills, and managing employees. It also involves remaining clinically current and responding to ever-changing licensing, insurance, and taxation laws that affect the practice.

Another critical personal characteristic relates to the practitioner's comfort with income ups and downs. Most private practitioners eventually arrive at a fairly steady income level, but even for veteran practitioners there are lean times when circumstances conspire to dramatically reduce income flow. How critical is it to you and your family that you have a guaranteed paycheck? Do you have the discipline to save for that inevitable lean time when your practice is slow--when your income is reduced but your business and living expenses remain?

Private practice requires an enormous commitment of time and energy. Are you prepared to work as long and as hard as it takes to make your practice become what you want? Many practitioners work 50-70 hours per week to establish their practice and then nearly as many when the practice becomes successful. Unlike working for an institution, there are no predetermined working hours, days on, or days off. Your work schedule is determined by listening to your own voice within. Paid vacations, paid sick days, and retirement accounts are never guaranteed for the private practitioner. Everything is dependent upon you and the success of your practice.

Finally, private practice is a risk! It is a risk that involves a substantial investment of financial and ego resources. People who are uncomfortable taking risks might want to carefully weigh the impact, on themselves and their families, of the uncertainties and ambiguities of private practice.

SUMMARY

This is a time of change and turmoil in private practice. Health care reform is dramatically altering the realities within private practice. The outcome is uncertain and will remain uncertain for several years to come. Regardless of the final outcome of health care reform, four variables should be considered when developing a private practice--the business structure of the practice, the clinical/client speciality, additional services, and the sources of payment. Net income from an established private practice can range up to $100,000 but the typical income is between $40,000 and $60,000 per year.

Private practice is rarely a suitable career choice for new inexperienced counselors. The challenges and risks associated with private practice are probably best left to veteran practitioners. The decision to pursue the establishment of a private practice should be based on a careful analysis of the market opportunities within a community and on the needs and preferences of the practitioner. Special consideration should be given to the unique demands of small business ownership. Ultimately, successful private practitioners must be both competent professionals and diligent managers of a business.

ADDITIONAL INFORMATION AND RESOURCES

Several professional associations can provide information about private practice and about private practitioners. Their addresses are listed in Appendix A:

American Counseling Association
American Mental Health Counselors Association
American Psychological Association

For additional reading, you might consider the following:

Browning, C. H. (1982). *Private practice handbook: The tools, tactics, and techniques for successful practice development (2nd ed.).* Los Alamitos, CA: Duncliff's International.

Klein, H. (Ed.) *Psychotherapy in private practice.* Binghampton, NY: Haworth Press, Inc. (A quarterly).

The Journal of Mental Health Counseling.

Psychotherapy Finances. Ridgewood, NJ: Ridgewood Financial Institute, Inc. (A monthly newsletter).

Chapter 7

CAREERS IN FEDERAL AND STATE AGENCIES

Andrew A. Helwig

Changes in legislation during the past few years, especially at the federal level, have had an impact on some of the traditional counseling occupations in federal and state agencies. For example, new law enforcement legislation is changing the occupation of parole officer and the Americans with Disabilities Act has influenced the role of the vocational rehabilitation counselor. In addition, a Department of Defense regulation has created a new position titled Transition Assistance Specialist to assist people leaving the armed forces.

These and other counseling and human services occupations are found in a variety of state and federally funded agencies. Federal dollars fund agencies such as vocational rehabilitation, public employment service (Job Service), and other employment and training programs falling under the *Job Training Partnership Act* (JTPA). Many state and federal agencies have positions such as counselor or psychologist.

There are many counselor and human services occupations at federal, state, or municipal government levels. Some of these are long-standing occupations--counselor, clinical psychologist, and social worker--principally at Veterans Affairs (VA) facilities and state hospitals. Other occupations are psychiatric technician or aide, drug and alcohol treatment specialist, job placement specialist, developmental disabilities specialist, veterans counselor, psychological services associate, and the more generic occupations of human services worker and mental health worker. Newer occupations funded by some governmental units include victim's advocate, independent adoptions specialist, and aging services representative.

Employment counseling and vocational rehabilitation counseling employ many workers. Because corrections is rapidly growing, the occupations of correction psychologist, case worker, correction counselor, parole officer, and youth counselor are explained in this chapter.   The military occupations of education counselor and transition assistance specialist are described.

EMPLOYMENT COUNSELOR

Places to Work

Employment counselors typically work for the Job Service, which is the public employment service in the United States. In most cases, the employment counselor is a state employee. Some employment counselors may be county or city employees, such as those who work in Service Delivery Areas under the JTPA umbrella.

Employment counselors may work in small rural community offices or large metropolitan offices with over 100 workers. There are over 2,000 state employment offices throughout the country, although not all of them have employment counselors. Individuals who do employment counseling may be called vocational or career counselors, Job Service Representatives, Job Service Specialists, or employment and training specialists. In some states, the employment counseling function has been all but eliminated with the exception of the counseling of veterans and some other special groups clearly identified by federal law. In some programs, the employment counselor may be called a case manager, youth specialist, dislocated worker specialist, or by some other title.

Colleagues at Work

The employment counselor works with a number of other professional staff persons. Most state employment offices have placement interviewers. There may also be workers specializing in employment services to veterans: these workers have titles such as veterans employment representative or disabled veterans outreach program specialist. In some Job Service offices applicants can file for unemployment insurance following layoff or job termination. In such offices, the employment counselor would also have contact with unemployment insurance claims representatives.   Employment counselors and JTPA case managers also work with instructors, social service agency staff, or vocational rehabilitation counselors in other agencies.

Whom Would You Help?

Employment counseling has traditionally been defined as assisting clients with problems of occupational choice, change, and adjustment. Clients may be young or old, from all socioeconomic levels, and of all racial and ethnic groups. State employment agencies and JTPA programs charge no fees for services provided; therefore, clients are often from lower socioeconomic levels. Other clients such as recent college graduates, military leavers and retirees, and mid-career changers also use the Job Service. Not many other counselors are able to work with as broad a range of clients as the employment counselor.

The range of applicants (clients) seeking employment counseling in state employment agencies and JTPA programs is extremely wide. It might be a 14-year-old youth seeking an after-school or summer job. It could be a 17-year-old dropout facing juvenile detention if he doesn't find work. It could be a 36-year-old unemployed woman in the process of divorce and anxious about supporting herself and her children. It might be a 52-year-old man terminated from a job after 25 years because a factory is closing or the company is reducing management staff. It may be a 72-year-old who is sick of retirement but needs help transferring her skills to a new job. JTPA clients are often economically disadvantaged.

Job Responsibilities

Many employment counselors assist people in choosing an occupation, changing a career, or adjusting to a new work environment. Others focus on assessing the need for training and developing a training plan. A helping relationship must be established so the client and counselor can accurately assess the situation. Formal assessment techniques such as aptitude and interest inventories may be used. If a career choice or change decision is to be made, the employment counselor needs to bring an assortment of information to the counseling process, including local and state labor market information, occupational trends and job demands, and information about employers. Information about training opportunities, vocational/technical programs, and private schools and colleges may be needed as well as admission requirements and financial aid data. Apprenticeship information may need to be provided and economically disadvantaged youth may be referred to Job Corp programs. Employment counselors also use computerized information resources.

In other instances, employment counselors may work with clients who have multiple barriers to employment. Clients may have a poor work history, lack skills, have a history of drug or alcohol abuse, or have personality characteristics that hinder them from finding or keeping a job. With such a client, the employment counselor may develop a plan to confront employability barriers. Supportive services from other community agencies are necessary to deal with some of the identified barriers to employment. Knowledge of community resources and the ability to work cooperatively with such agencies is critical. The employment counselor may work as a case manager ensuring that a variety of services are provided the client.

Employment counselors must relate to and establish relationships with a broad range of clients. They should be sensitive to and understand individual differences. Awareness of gender issues and consideration of clients for nontraditional occupations is expected. Employment counselors should be flexible, patient, and able to handle frustrations due to working with difficult clients, poor working conditions in some offices, or assignment of non-counseling duties. Tolerance for administrative procedures and record keeping is helpful.

Education, Training, and Salary

States have considerable autonomy regarding the education and experience requirements of applicants for employment counselor positions. Substituting related work experience for some educational requirements is often possible. Consequently, some entry-level employment counselor positions may be filled by individuals with a bachelor's degree or less. The educational standard for a journeyman employment counselor, as specified by the profession, is a master's degree in counseling or a closely related field.

JTPA programs administered by cities or counties have even more latitude in the education and training requirements for employment counselors or case managers. Often, work experience is more valued than education.

Annual starting salaries for employment counselors who work for state employment agencies range from $22,000 to $30,000. In city or in county government agencies administering JTPA programs, the lower end of the range may be $15,000.

CORRECTION PSYCHOLOGIST AND CORRECTION COUNSELOR

Places to Work

Psychologists and counselors employed in corrections are likely to work in state and federal prisons, including penitentiaries, correctional institutions, prison camps, and prison medical facilities. At the federal level, these institutions are characterized as minimum, low, medium or high in security requirements. Facilities housing juvenile offenders, primarily at the state level, may also employ psychologists and counselors.

In the federal system, in addition to psychologists, case managers provide many services to inmates. The counselor in the federal system works with inmates on a day-to-day basis to make sure the inmate follows a rehabilitation plan. In state correction agencies, a counselor may be a trained social worker or licensed professional counselor.

Colleagues at Work

Correction psychologists, case managers, and counselors work with a variety of human services staff including program administrators, parole officers, and other specialists such as drug and alcohol counselors, recreation therapists, teachers, and psychiatrists. The amount of contact with correctional officers (prison guards) varies. Case managers and counselors are also likely to have regular contact with social service staff, employment specialists, half-way house staff, and family members of inmates.

Whom Would You Help?

At the federal level, 93% of inmates are male. Whites and blacks are represented in about equal numbers (35%), 26% are Hispanic, with the rest from other racial groups. Seventy-six percent of inmates are U.S. citizens and average inmate age is 37. Sixty-one percent of federal inmates have been sentenced for drug offenses and 10% for robbery.   Prison terms of federal and state inmates may range from a few months to life; some state inmates are on "death row" and scheduled for execution.

Correction psychologists accept inmate referrals from case managers, counselors, and others in the prison system. Inmates may show symptoms of chronic mental illness including schizophrenia and depression. Inmates who experience situational adjustment difficulties or alcohol or other drug abuse may be referred to correctional psychologists.   All inmates in an institution are potentially on a counselor's caseload.

Job Responsibilities of Psychologists

Job responsibilities of correction psychologists include comprehensive evaluations using a wide variety of psychological procedures and techniques.   The psychologist develops and implements a treatment program that may include individual and group therapy. Often the psychologist is asked to perform consultative and advisory duties and may guide others in the application of a therapeutic plan. Supervision of other psychologists and perhaps other human services staff may be expected. It is common for the psychologist to develop and conduct staff training for institution personnel. A significant responsibility of the correction psychologist is completing paperwork. This documentation might include inmate contact forms, case disposition forms, psychological reports, and group therapy rosters. The psychologist may also be responsible for some security functions including escorting inmates from one location to another and recording entry and exit from the facility.

Job Responsibilities of Counselors and Case Managers

The counselor's or case manager's responsibilities include a variety of duties using casework and group and individual counseling methods and techniques to help inmates adjust to institutional living.   The counselor helps inmates in solving social, economic, and emotional problems with the goal of changing their attitudes and behavior. Counselors may work with groups of inmates who are sex offenders, those who have drug and alcohol problems, and others with issues of anger management. Counselors also promote the development of a sense of dignity and responsibility. The counselor is a liaison between the inmate, the rest of the institution, and the outside world--including courts and parole boards. The counselor may help the inmate handle day-to-day adjustment problems, grievances, and legal issues.

The correction counselor, often with other staff, develops an individual performance or treatment plan to include such issues as academic or vocational training; employment; and social, economic, and behavioral adjustments. Counselors are responsible for a periodic performance review of the inmates on their caseload. They may also be responsible for classification reviews (e.g., change in security level from maximum to medium) and parole plans. The correction counselor may expect to process a large amount of paperwork. Conflict is also possible between the role of the counselor (e.g., helper) and the role of law enforcement agent (e.g., disciplinarian). The counselor functions within strict security requirements of the institution and, in some settings, must demonstrate proficiency with a firearm at regular intervals.

Personal Characteristics

Correction psychologists and counselors must be able to handle stress and be fair, firm, and consistent. They should have no major unresolved personal issues. They need to be even-tempered, objective, and able to deal with inmates' anger, sarcasm, and other antisocial behaviors. They should be able to use confrontation skills and not be vulnerable to manipulation. Psychologists and counselors must treat each inmate as a unique individual but be careful not to over identify with an inmate. Awareness of the symptoms of burnout is important.

Education, Training, and Salary

Correction psychologists have a PhD or PsyD and may or may not be required to be licensed as psychologists by the state. Some states require licensure within a specified time frame. In some states, there are positions in corrections titled psychological services associate, or clinical behavioral specialist. Such positions usually require a master's degree in psychology. Case managers in the federal system have at least a bachelor's degree with academic credits in the social sciences, although many of them have master's degrees. In state prison systems, counselors may have bachelor or higher degrees and many of them are social workers or licensed professional counselors. In the federal system, counselors typically come from correctional officer (prison guard) ranks and help manage inmates on a day-to-day basis.

The starting salary for entry-level correction psychologists with a PhD range from $28,000 to $38,000, depending on the state. Counseling psychologists who work in the federal correction system would begin at the GS-11 level, with a starting salary of over $36,000.

Correction counselors' entry-level salaries at state institutions range from $20,000 to $26,000. Federal case managers who have a bachelor's degree and at least one year of experience usually begin employment at the GS-9 level, which has a starting salary of about $30,000.

YOUTH COUNSELOR

In the corrections system, the youth counselor assists in the rehabilitation and social development of delinquent youth. In addition to youth counselors, many state correctional systems will have other non-professional positions such as youth services worker or youth development aide.

Places to Work

Youth counselors work in juvenile institutions that often focus on academic (high school) preparation. Some facilities are characterized as treatment oriented while others are detention oriented with minimal treatment. Other youth counselors work in group homes, halfway houses, or outdoor camps.

Colleagues at Work

Youth counselors work closely with youth services workers or aides, if these positions exist in the correctional system, and with correctional officers (guards). Other colleagues include treatment team coordinators (usually in a supervisory position), case managers, program administrators, and teachers. Relationships may also be established with family members of delinquents, attorneys, psychologists, employment specialists, and other community agency staff.

Whom Would You Help?

The age range of juveniles in an institution may be 13 to 19. You might work with a 17-year old boy who has been convicted for car theft or a 15-year-old runaway girl convicted for selling drugs. Youngsters convicted of violent crimes such as assault or drive-by shootings may also be held in juvenile institutions.

Typically, the facility is not coeducational. Following conviction for a crime, most juveniles are placed on probation. With subsequent offenses, placement in a juvenile facility is likely. Consequently, most youth in a juvenile institution are multiple offenders for whom probation was not a sufficient punishment to stop them from committing additional offenses.

Job Responsibilities

Usually all facets of the youth's life are supervised by youth counselors including their educational, work, and recreational activities. The youth counselor is responsible for maintaining discipline and socially desirable behavior in accordance with a prescribed treatment or performance plan. The youth counselor may also provide instruction or guidance regarding personal hygiene, nutrition, and dress.

In treatment centers, the youth counselor may provide individual and group counseling. These services may focus on special areas such as drug and alcohol or anger management. The youth counselor works closely with other staff members, families of the juvenile, and staff of other agencies. Periodic and special written evaluation reports are necessary. Routine record keeping is also required. Youth counselors are responsible for security; they enforce policies and regulations and help search for and return runaways.

Personal Characteristics

Youth counselors must be patient and exercise good judgment. They must be advocates for youth and be able to work effectively with youth from a variety of racial, ethnic, and social backgrounds. Maturity is a valuable trait. Because some juveniles exhibit provocative (hostile, abusive, assaultive) behavior, youth counselors must exercise self-control and restraint. They must be able to handle the stress which is associated with volatile situations. The ability to recognize small positive behavior changes and reinforce them is helpful. The youth counselor should also be able to respond quickly and effectively in emergencies.

Education, Training, and Salary

Depending on the state and the specific job duties, requirements for entry level professional youth counselors may range from several years of related experience to a college degree. Many positions are filled by master's level trained individuals.

The starting salary for youth counselors ranges from $22,000 to 32,000.

PROBATION OFFICER

The probation officer performs professional-level work supervising probationers and parolees. A probationer is a convicted offender whose sentence has been suspended, whereas a parolee is a prisoner who has been conditionally released for a specified period of time. In some units of government, probation officer and parole officer are separate occupations. In federal corrections both functions are performed by the same individual; however, as a consequence of recent federal legislative changes, individuals convicted for federal violations fall under the jurisdiction of the court system rather than a parole office. Consequently, the federal system will only have probation officers. The following description of a probation officer includes parole officer duties.

Places to Work

Probation officers may work for federal, state, county, or municipal agencies. Their office is usually in the community they serve, although some probation officers are employed at correctional institutions. It is not unusual for probation and parole officers to spend up to one-half of their time out of their offices and "on the streets."

Colleagues at Work

Probation officers work with other law enforcement personnel, including police, attorneys, and judges. They work closely with a variety of specialists who work with their clients. Therapists, teachers, and staff members of a variety of community agencies are their colleagues. The nature of their work also puts them in contact with family members, friends, and employers of their clients. Federal probation officers may work with Secret Service and FBI agents.

Whom Would You Help?

The probation officer may work with probationers who are individuals adjudicated by a court of law. Because of the nature of the crime or extenuating circumstances, such as a first offense, the individual may be placed on probation or receive a suspended sentence with probation. Examples of individuals on probation are the woman convicted of prostitution for the first time or the man convicted of embezzling $5,000 from his employer. Parolees are individuals released conditionally from a correctional institution. If they meet the conditions of their parole for the period of time specified, they cease to be under the control of the court system. An example of a parolee may be a man released from jail after spending time for vehicular homicide or a woman released after serving time for being an accomplice in an armed robbery. Crimes committed by probationers and parolees may range from petty theft to multiple murders.

Job Responsibilities

The overall responsibility of probation officers is to supervise closely the activities of their clients to ensure that they meet the conditions of probation or parole. The probation officer determines what services, including counseling, might be helpful in assisting probationers or parolees. Probation officers assist their clients in their personal, social, and economic adjustment in the community in order for them to become good citizens.

The probation officer must perform considerable investigatory work, although in the federal system, the emphasis has shifted from investigations to supervision. Investigations may be necessary prior to the development of a pre-parole plan or after a probation or parole violation occurs. Many of the probation or parole officer's activities terminate in paperwork.

Probation officers work closely with employers, educational institutions, and other community agencies that may provide services to their clients such as psychotherapy and alcohol/drug counseling. Probation officers may be required to gather urine samples from some clients for drug screening.

Electronic monitoring, including home confinement, is an increasingly popular method of restricting activities of probationers and parolees. In some agencies, one-fourth or more individuals may be electronically monitored which may ease the probation or parole officer's supervision requirements; however, the size of their caseloads may increase.

In some governmental units, the parole officer is considered a law enforcement officer and carries a badge and a gun. The parole officer can make arrests when parole violations are indicated and then has the responsibility for prosecuting the individual. Probation officers usually do not carry a weapon although in the federal system it is an option if the officer has received weapons training.

Personal Characteristics

Probation officers must have strong listening and communication skills. They should be mature, exercise sound judgment, and be able to make decisions. They should possess integrity, be even-tempered, and have no major personal problems. They should be able to work independently and be organized and articulate. Probation officers should enjoy challenging work assignments (occasionally dangerous ones), and be concerned for their clients. Probation officers must be aware of the manipulative tactics of some clients and have a healthy skepticism leading to the need to "always verify" what the client says.

Education, Training, and Salary

A bachelor's degree is the usual educational requirement for probation officers although, in some instances, experience can be substituted for some education. In the federal system, the entry level probation officer must have a bachelor's degree in a social science field and one year of experience. The majority of federal probation officers have a master's degree.

At the state level, starting salaries for probation and parole officers may range from $20,000 to $26,000. Federal probation officers typically begin work at the GS-9 level ($30,000) before moving to the GS-11 level ($36,200).

VOCATIONAL REHABILITATION COUNSELOR

Places to Work

State vocational rehabilitation agencies receive approximately 80% of their funding from federal sources. Rehabilitation counselors in such state agencies work in a variety of settings. Most work in offices that may be shared with other state staff from such agencies as social services or employment services. Vocational rehabilitation counselors may be stationed in a state hospital, university campus, Job Service office, or local school district. Others may work at sheltered workshops. Opportunities for vocational rehabilitation counselors in private agencies are rapidly expanding.

Colleagues at Work

The usual coworkers of a vocational rehabilitation counselor are other counselors, clerical support staff, and supervisory staff. Vocational rehabilitation counselors regularly work with a variety of professionals from several agencies, including physicians, psychologists, social workers, instructors/trainers, and employment service staff. Many vocational rehabilitation counselors also work directly with employers.

Whom Would You Help?

Clients eligible for rehabilitation services have physical or mental limitations or both.   Individuals often have a combination of handicapping conditions with additional problems such as alcohol abuse. Because of limited financial resources, priority for providing services to potential clients may need to be determined based on the severity of handicapping conditions.   Examples of vocational rehabilitation clients are the 35-year-old woman who developed multiple sclerosis or the 48-year-old man who suffered an industrial accident, must now change occupations, and is also depressed. Clients range from teenagers to older adults and come from all socioeconomic and ability levels.

Job Responsibilities

The goal of vocational rehabilitation counseling is to assist eligible clients to reach a successful status. Successful closures usually mean employment in a regular job or sheltered workplace, becoming an independent homemaker, or helping in a family business (even without pay).

The vocational rehabilitation counselor is a case manager working with many clients. The counselor proceeds from a comprehensive assessment to the development of a rehabilitation plan appropriate for the client. This is followed by counseling and related activities to assure successful accomplishment of the plan. The counselor arranges for medical, psychological, and vocational examinations and gathers additional data as necessary. To assist the client, the vocational rehabilitation counselor can purchase services and materials such as prosthetic devices, special equipment, tools, and uniforms. Payment for education or training is also possible.

The *Americans With Disabilities Act* has helped educate employers about their responsibilities regarding individuals with handicapping conditions. The counselor works closely with employers to facilitate training and job placement and consults with employers about job accommodations necessary to employ an individual with handicapping conditions.

The vocational rehabilitation counselor is responsible for the completion of ongoing written narratives, contract forms for services, letters, and other documentation for accountability. Most counselors will also visit other agency staff and follow up with service providers.

Personal Characteristics

Vocational rehabilitation counselors must be able to establish helping relationships with clients who have a wide variety of handicapping conditions. They must guard against becoming overly invested with a client; remaining objective is necessary. Vocational counselors need strong analytical skills to make use of assessment and evaluation data from multiple sources. They must be able to work with many clients at one time, so organizational skills are critical. Because of the necessary contacts with many resource providers as well as employers, vocational rehabilitation counselors should have the ability to negotiate on behalf of their clients.

Education, Training, and Salary

A bachelor's degree and experience in vocational rehabilitation is required for entry-level positions in many state vocational rehabilitation offices. Some states require a master's degree. The professional credential in this field is Certified Rehabilitation Counselor (CRC) but ordinarily not required for entry-level employment.

Entry-level salaries for state vocational rehabilitation counselors range from $22,000 to $28,000 and will vary depending upon degree and experience.

MILITARY TRANSITION ASSISTANCE SPECIALIST

Places to Work

Transition assistance specialists or counselors work in programs established in the early 1990s by the Department of Defense in all branches of the military. These positions were created as a consequence of the ending of the "cold war" and the subsequent reduction in the size of the military and the desire to help military members make a successful transition into the civilian world. Transition assistance specialists may be found on most military bases, hospitals, or aircraft carriers. They are located at overseas bases as well.

Colleagues at Work

Depending upon the branch of the military and structure of the office, the transition assistance specialist works with many other colleagues who usually perform specialized functions. In the Air Force, Navy, and Marines, the transition assistance program is located in Family Support Centers. In the Army, it is part of the Army Career Alumni Program. Colleagues might be educational counselors, marriage counselors, drug and alcohol specialists, testing technicians, computer technicians (to help run national resume and job search programs), and clerical support staff. Besides these personnel, transition assistance specialists work with Veterans Affairs, vocational rehabilitation, employment service, and vocational-technical and community college staff.

Whom Would You Help?

Transition assistance staff help military personnel who are from six months to one-and-a-half years from completing their military duties due to completion of tour of duty, retirement, or other discharge. An Individual Transition Plan (ITP) is developed to facilitate the person's successful move into the civilian world following the military commitment. Examples of individuals eligible for transition services would be the Marine who has completed 20 years of service and will be "retiring" at the age of 41, or the 23 year-old woman who has decided that she is only interested in one tour of duty in the Army, or the 34 year-old Air Force specialist whose goal was to make a career of the military but is told that, because of reductions in troop strength, he will no longer have a position after his current tour expires.

Job Responsibilities

Following completion of the ITP, the transition assistance specialist works with the individual to implement the plan, providing information and serving as a referral agent. Most transition programs conduct two- to four-day workshops that address a variety of issues suitable to the transitioning military member. Separation services and benefits are identified. Often staff from Veterans Affairs, Job Service, and other agencies participate in the workshops. The individual is encouraged and assisted in identifying skills which transfer from the military to civilian employment. Job search, resume preparation, and interviewing techniques are topics covered in the workshops as well as in individual and group counseling.

A variety of automated services are available to the individual in transition. A national computerized search and resumé service which employers may access can be used. National job information is available on computer that includes openings of private employers and public and community agencies. Job listings from the Job Service may be available. Some offices have computerized guidance information systems such as DISCOVER and SIGI PLUS. Interest and ability testing may be available and assistance in completing the Federal Application may be provided.

Referral to other services is common. Individuals needing personal, marriage, financial, or other services are referred to appropriate specialists. Others may be referred to the education counselor. On Army bases, the Job Assistance Center is available for direct employment assistance.

Personal Characteristics

The transition assistance specialist must have an interest in and concern for people. Listening and communication skills are necessary as is the ability to communicate in group situations. The ability to work with people from a variety of backgrounds is helpful. A wide range of employment experiences, both civilian and military, will give the transition assistance specialist insight in working with transitioning military personnel. Computer literacy is helpful and the transition assistance specialist must be willing to work in a regulated environment.

Education, Training, and Salary

The usual entry level education is a bachelor's degree with some course work in the social sciences although work experience can sometimes substitute for a degree. Many transition assistance specialists have master's degrees although not necessarily in counseling or psychology.

Transition assistance specialists are civilians working on military bases who fall under the General Schedule pay structure. The entry level for most such positions is GS-9 ($30,000). Managers or supervisors of transition assistance programs are typically at the GS-11 level ($36,200).

MILITARY EDUCATION COUNSELOR

Places to Work

The military education counselor works on military bases, naval stations, and military hospitals in the United States and overseas. Small military facilities may not have their own education counselor but could be served by one who travels from place to place. Education counselors may be placed in units called a campus (e.g., Navy Campus) or in an Education Center.

Colleagues at Work

Education counselors are civilian Department of Defense (DOD) personnel. Typically, their colleagues at work are also civilian personnel and include clerical assistants, a testing examiner, and a supervisor. In the Army and Air Force, the education counselor's occupational title is guidance counselor and their supervisor is an educational services officer. In the Navy and Marines, the education counselor's official title is educational services specialist. In the Marines, some educational services specialists are members of the military, not civilians.

Education counselors work closely with admissions and instructional personnel of colleges who have authority to teach on military bases. Referrals may be made to family services and to transition and employment services.

Whom Would You Help?

Education counselors work primarily with active duty military personnel. The majority of a counselor's military clients are enlisted personnel, although they also work with officers. Education counselors also help civilians who are employed by the Department of Defense and work at the military facility. Dependents of military personnel are also eligible for services. For example, the client might be a newly enlisted member who would like to begin pursuing a bachelor's degree while in the military. Or, perhaps the client is a civilian worker on base who wants to pursue a field of study but local schools and colleges do not offer what the worker wants. In this case, the education counselor can help arrange for study in an external degree program through distance learning.

The military personnel with whom the counselor works may be an individual relatively new to the service, another nearing completion of the required period of enlistment and soon leaving the service, or another retiring from the military with 20 or more years of service. The civilians and dependents with whom the military counselor works have a wide range of ability levels and represent many cultures and countries.

Job Responsibilities

Education counselors usually identify education or training opportunities outside the military that will enhance their client's military career or help prepare them for a post-military career. Sometimes career or vocational counseling is necessary before appropriate educational opportunities can be identified.

Enlisted personnel who plan a career in the military are encouraged to complete college-level courses, or earn an associate of arts or a bachelor's degree to enhance promotional possibilities. To help ensure successful careers in the military, officers are encouraged to complete a master's degree.

Education counselors assist their clients in identifying appropriate courses or colleges (sometimes correspondence courses), assist them in applying for admission to college, and help them process tuition assistance requests if appropriate. They also help them evaluate their military training and experience to determine if college credit can be obtained for them. The College Level Examination Program (CLEP) is administered through their office.

Education counselors may also be responsible for other tests administered through the educational service office. Some offices administer the General Educational Development (GED) exam, the Scholastic Aptitude Test (SAT), the Graduate Record Exam (GRE), and Graduate Management Admissions Test (GMAT).

The education counselor may participate in the 2-3 day transition assistance workshops for military personnel who are separating from the military. These workshops address such issues as employment-seeking skills, resumé writing, educational opportunities, and financial aid. Retirement briefings may also be the responsibility of the education counselor.

In the Navy, the education counselor may be responsible for assessing the educational needs of military personnel and then contracting with colleges and other institutions to provide the training following a request for proposal review process. Other duties of education counselors may include promotion and publicity efforts and education fairs.

Personal Characteristics

Education counselors must have a desire to help people and a concern for their growth and development. Counselors are in a position to expand the educational possibilities of their clients. They do this through their ability to relate to individuals of all cultural and ability levels and through their knowledge of educational and other opportunities. Education counselors must be well-organized and pay attention to detail. Desirable personal characteristics include patience, dedication, and the ability to stay motivated and knowledgeable of possibilities for their clients.

Education, Training, and Salary

The minimum education level for military education counselor is a bachelor's degree although many begin with a master's degree. Because the military branches view the education services offered as voluntary (not required of military personnel), financial support for these education offices is weak. As civilian employees of the Department of Defense (DOD), military counselors are paid in accordance with the General Schedule. The levels for military counselor range from GS-5 to GS-11. A GS-5 individual with a bachelor's degree would begin at about $20,000. With a master's degree, military counselors would usually be at the GS-9 level which has a starting salary of about $30,000.

ADDITIONAL INFORMATION AND RESOURCES

As indicated earlier, these are just a few of the counseling and human services occupations found in federal and state agencies. Additional information about these and other occupations may be found in the suggested readings or requested directly from the agencies mentioned in the chapter. Information can also be obtained from the *Occupational Outlook Handbook* (OOH) or from the associations named below (Addresses may be found in the Appendix):

> American Association for Adult and Continuing Education
> American Correctional Association
> American Psychological Association
> American Rehabilitation Counseling Association
> Association for Counselors and Educators in Government
> Commission of Rehabilitation Counselor Certification
> Federal Probation Officers Association
> International Association of Addiction and Offender Counselors
> National Council on Rehabilitation Education
> National Employment Counseling Association
> National Rehabilitation Counseling Association

The following references may be helpful:

Champion, D. J. (1990) *Probation and parole in the United States.* New York: Merrill.

Gibson, R. L., & Mitchell, M. H. (1990). *Introduction to counseling and guidance (3rd ed.).* New York: MacMillan.

Gladding, S. T. (1992). *Counseling: A counseling profession (2nd ed.).* New York: Merrill.

Meyers, D., Helwig, A., Gjernes, O., & Chickering, J. (1985). The National Employment Counselors Association. *Journal of Counseling and Development, 63,* 440-443.

Palone, J. J. (1994). *Young victims, young offenders.* Binghamton, NY: The Haworth Press.

Chapter 8

CAREERS IN
HEALTH CARE FACILITIES

Nancy J. Garfield
Jeannie Beaman

Treatment is provided at health care facilities to people with both acute (immediate, short term) and chronic (long term, repetitive) illnesses. There are a number of types of health care facilities, and many different health care providers work in these settings. Work settings represented in this chapter include the community hospital or medical center, rehabilitation centers, nursing homes, psychiatric facilities, and Veterans Affairs Medical Centers (VAs). Other health care facilities not discussed include hospices, mental retardation facilities, single-day surgery centers, children's hospitals, and substance abuse facilities.

People who are being treated at one of these facilities are called patients or clients, and may be seen as inpatients--people who are admitted to stay at the facility for a period of time; or outpatients-- people who come to the facility to receive service and then go home. Patients are hospitalized and treated as inpatients when their problem or illness requires more intensive treatment and supervision by health care professionals.

People who want to help others in a health care facility might have one of the following occupations: physician, psychologist, counselor, psychiatrist, social worker, pharmacist, physical therapist, occupational therapist, or dietician. These professionals make up what is called a "treatment team." This team works together to provide coordinated programs to help the patient recover as fully and quickly as possible. Treatment team members may not all meet together to develop treatment plans, but usually a group of core professionals will meet to set goals for the patient. The team may be made up of only the physician and nurse, or include a number of the professionals mentioned above. Each team member contributes information from his or her own area of expertise to enhance patient care.

Different work settings serve different purposes. Hospitals provide medical care for a variety of problems that range from the delivery of a baby to organ transplants. Veterans Affairs hospitals, the largest single health care facility nationwide, provide medical and psychiatric treatment for veterans. Psychiatric facilities treat patients who have a psychiatric illness and have difficulty functioning in the community. Problems treated in a psychiatric facility may include chronic depression, psychosis (delusions and hallucinations), substance abuse, or Post-Traumatic Stress Disorder. Rehabilitation facilities provide treatment for people who need care while they recover or recuperate from an illness or accident. Patients may receive inpatient or outpatient treatment from these facilities.

Nursing homes serve a different purpose. Often people who are unable to care for themselves after an illness, accident, or surgery reside in nursing homes for a short period of time while recovering. Nursing homes also care for elderly or infirm people who can no longer live by themselves and need someone to supervise their activities of daily living such as bathing, taking medication, eating balanced meals, or generally care for themselves.

There are many types of health care settings. People in the helping professions work in a variety of settings, and have a variety of ways to help people help themselves.

CHARACTERISTICS OF PEOPLE WHO WORK IN HEALTH CARE SETTINGS

Professionals who work in health care settings need to have the following characteristics. They should be able to:

- work with patients and staff of various ethnicities, cultures, socio-economic groups, genders, abilities, handicapping conditions, and sexual orientations;
- write well to document care provided or treatment needed;
- work with professionals of other disciplines to provide coordinated care;
- be responsible and trusted to carry out treatment orders for patient care;

- listen to patient concerns and convey those concerns to other professionals as needed;
- comprehend what other professionals have written about the patient's condition;
- follow directions, to work as a team member; and
- set boundaries; to maintain objectivity, not getting overly engaged in the care of the patient, or becoming emotionally involved with the patient and thus unable to provide quality patient care.

TRENDS

There are changes or trends in health care delivery that all providers of health care should follow. Health care delivery is being shaped by insurance carriers who are trying to provide quality service at lower cost. Many people now receive care under a "managed care system." Managed care has, in many cases, changed the way health care is delivered by requiring that patients must first see their primary care provider (physician) who coordinates their care and decides if the patient needs to see a specialist for a problem. For example, if a child has asthma, and needs treatment for a flare-up of the asthmatic condition, the parents would not go directly to the asthma specialist. Rather, they will need to take the child to the primary care provider, usually a pediatrician or family practitioner, to get permission and a referral to the asthma specialist. Thus, the primary care provider serves as a gatekeeper, assuring that only those who need specialized treatment are referred to the more costly specialists.

A second trend in health care has been to provide as much care as possible on an outpatient basis. Health care providers hospitalize their patients as short a period of time as possible. Treating patients as outpatients is less costly, and often as effective, as treating them for extended periods of time as inpatients. There has also been a trend to provide a variety of medical services or procedures on an outpatient basis.

SOCIAL WORKERS

Social workers provide a variety of services in the facilities mentioned in this chapter. Social workers in any of these settings (medical, psychiatric, rehabilitation, or nursing home) almost always work with other professionals and health care providers on a multi disciplinary team.

Social workers with a Bachelor of Social Work (BSW) degree are often hired to do "case management." Case management is defined by the National Association of Social Workers (NASW) as "providing services whereby a professional social worker assesses the needs of the client and the client's family, when appropriate, and arranges, coordinates, monitors, evaluates, and advocates for a package of multiple services to meet the specific client's complex needs." A social worker or case manager would do initial screening or intake assessments; patient and family education; crisis intervention; assist patients and family with adjustment to illness, disability, hospitalization, and/or nursing home placement; consultation with other team members, hospital staff, nursing home staff, and community resources. Additionally, the case manager would be involved in discharge planning; coordinating care after discharge; money management; assessment of need for a guardian; assessing housing needs; locating adequate housing; assisting patients in learning problem solving skills; assisting with vocational, educational, and legal issues; and assessing substance abuse problems and family care-giving problems (caring for children, an ill spouse, or an aging parent).

A social worker with a Master of Social Work (MSW) degree is usually referred to as a "clinical social worker." The clinical social worker has additional knowledge of human behavior, interpersonal relationships, health/social service systems, and community resources. The master's-level social worker would do psychosocial assessments and provide psychosocial diagnoses; provide individual, group, and marital/family therapy; provide grief counseling and crisis intervention; make and coordinate discharge and aftercare planning; provide case management and care coordination; give supervisory assistance to less experienced social workers; furnish consultative assistance to clinical and administrative colleagues; advocate for the client; serve on quality assurance review teams; participate in policy and program planning; and participate in social work research.

In larger organizations, an MSW degree is required for an administrative position or chief of a department. The Doctorate of Social Work (DSW) is most often the entry level for teaching, writing, and research. The trend is for states to require both the appropriate college degree and a license before one can practice social work. Both the BSW and MSW have licensing exams which can be taken after the degree is awarded.

Clinical social workers with an MSW and two years of clinical experience may take a licensing exam that allows them to practice as independent practitioners in private practice. Different states have different titles for this level of license, but it is generally referred to as the Licensed Specialist Clinical Social Worker (LSCSW). All levels of social work licenses require continuing education units (CEUs) to maintain the license.

Annual salaries for BSW degree social workers average $20,000. MSW annual salaries range from $25,600 to $38,700.

PSYCHOLOGISTS

Psychologists in health care settings work with people who have emotional or psychological problems. Psychologists use interviews, tests, observation, and other means to assess how to help those seeking assistance. One of the major tools of psychologists is assessment. Psychologists may use tests of personality, intelligence, aptitude, interests, and cognitive functioning to better understand their clients. With the results of these data they help develop treatment plans, make recommendations to the treatment team, and make suggestions to the client about what might help the client resolve his or her problems.

Psychologists provide therapy to individuals and groups. They may help the client solve a specific problem, such as what field of study to major in, if a divorce is in their best interest, or how they might begin to be less depressed. They also may work with clients on more global problems, such as being more assertive, stopping smoking, or stopping drug or alcohol abuse.

Psychologists in health care settings help diagnose the patient's problems, formulate treatment goals, and provide treatment. Psychologists may be generalists, who are able to work with people of differing ages with differing problems, or specialists, focusing on one particular form of diagnosis or treatment. Health psychologists help people adjust to medical problems such as a diagnosis of cancer, use of dialysis, or health related problems such as smoking or obesity. They may promote good health through stress management or they might work with patients who experience sexual dysfunction.

Neuropsychologists asses how the brain functions and the relationship of brain function to behavior. They develop rehabilitative programs for people with brain damage to help them overcome the results of their injury or illness (e.g., stroke, cancer, closed head injury). Child psychologists specialize in the diagnosis and treatment of childhood disorders.

Psychology careers that are expected to grow faster than normal in the next decade include health psychology, neuropsychology, and geropsychology (assessment and treatment of the problems of aging individuals and their families). Many psychologists have clinical privileges to treat patients in a hospital and also see patients as outpatients in a community mental health center or private practice. Individual private practice of psychology is changing as a viable full-time option as health care reform evolves [see Chapter 6].

Most psychologists working in health care facilities have completed a doctoral degree and are licensed to practice independently. In some states, masters level psychologists may work at state facilities such as state psychiatric hospitals or facilities for the mentally retarded.

Doctoral level psychologists' salaries range from $35,000 to $70,000 per year and the median annual salary for master's degree graduates is $34,000.

PSYCHOLOGY TECHNICIANS

Psychology technicians work under the direction and supervision of a licensed psychologist. They may have a bachelor's degree (most common) or a master's degree in psychology or a related social science field. Psychology technicians help psychologists by doing activities such as administering and scoring objective psychological tests (multiple choice), gathering data for reports or research, leading psychoeducational groups or classes, or completing statistical reports. People who are "psych techs" perform activities that require attention to detail, sensitivity to others, and ability to work as part of a team. Psych techs usually work in large facilities doing testing, recording data, and generally helping psychologists provide services to patients. Salaries for psych techs range from $18,300 to $37,000 depending on degree earned, years of experience, and job.

COUNSELORS

Counselors working in health care facilities generally have a masters or doctoral degree. At the masters and doctoral level, counselors will have completed course work that helps them understand human dynamics and how to help people. Masters level counselors will have had several courses (practica) where they work with clients under the supervision of a licensed professional. Doctoral level counselors will have had an additional 60 semester hours of course work with more supervised practica or internships and more course work in understanding the individual, group dynamics, etc. In many settings, counselors are a part of the treatment team, providing assistance via individual and group treatment. Counselors with generalist training may provide assistance to people with emotional problems or they may have received specialist training in areas such as substance abuse, problems of the elderly, or work with children.

There are many associate degree programs and an increasing number of bachelor's degree programs which provide training to people who want to be substance abuse counselors. People with the associate's degree have completed approximately 60 hours of course work, including studying human behavior and information about he effects of substance abuse. Many substance abuse counselors are "recovering" abusers (they have been substance abusers but are no longer using substances of abuse), or members of families where there was substance abuse. Substance abuse counselors generally have completed practica or field experience by observing substance abuse treatment in a community treatment center. Substance abuse counselors may be credentialed by the National Alcohol and Drug Addiction Counselors Association. Most states also license or credential substance abuse counselors.

Salaries of full time educational and vocational counselors may range from $20,000 to $52,000, depending on degree, years in the position, and work setting. Substance abuse counselors' average salary is $27,000, with salary ranging from $23,000 to $33,000, depending on education, years of experience, and credentialing.

REHABILITATION COUNSELORS

People who have had severe illness or injury may need both physical help in learning how to do tasks of daily living, e.g., dressing, eating, walking; and psychological assistance in coping with the physical and emotional changes that accompany a change in physical or intellectual functioning. Rehabilitation counselors work with patients who have had a physical or psychological problem and need assistance to return to independent functioning and work. They are often employed by a medical or psychiatric facility. Rehabilitation counselors may work at community agencies such as state vocational rehabilitation, helping people who were injured on the job or are recovering from an illness and can no longer do the work they did before. These professionals may coordinate remedial education services; supervise a sheltered workshop, where the patient can be assessed for job-related strengths and weaknesses; provide counseling about the implications of the illness or injury on day-to-day functioning; and help the patients discuss their thoughts and feelings about their changes in functioning and make plans for the future.

Rehabilitation counselors complete a masters degree in counseling or rehabilitation counseling. Rehabilitation course work would include classes in disability determination, rehabilitation, psychology of illness or disability, human dynamics and psychopathology, and practical experience (practica) working with people needing rehabilitation services. Rehabilitation counselors' salaries are a function of level of education, work setting, and years in the field. Salaries may range from $18,000 to over $50,000 depending on these variables.

THERAPISTS USING ARTISTIC MEDIA

It has long been known that the use of artistic media may help some individuals when "traditional" talking methods do not. Use of art, music, drama, dance, horticulture, and ceramics are only a few ways individuals may express themselves in a non-talking mode. Often patients need a different medium to communicate how they are feeling, to achieve a sense of accomplishment, or to express emotions. People in these fields are able to combine their expertise with the media (e.g., growing plants, painting and drawing, making things out of clay, or playing an instrument or singing) and their desire to help others feel better about themselves, resolve problems, or learn how to communicate with others.

Therapists who work with different media generally have training both in the artistic media and in understanding and helping people. Minimally, they complete a bachelor's degree in their field and, for many of the specialities, the master's degree is the entry-level degree. Completion of the degree includes academic courses about their media, learning about the dynamics of people, courses in psychology, and a practicum experience where they work in a setting using their media to help others while under the supervision of an experienced therapist. These specialists may work at inpatient facilities such as psychiatric hospitals, rehabilitation centers, and nursing homes, or provide services on an outpatient basis as part of a comprehensive clinic or community mental health center. Some therapists may provide services on a contractual basis and are paid by the hour. Salaries may range from $15,000 to $35,000 depending on education, work setting, and work responsibilities.

PHYSICIANS

Physicians may be employed by a health care facility or work in an individual or group practice in the community and have admitting and treating privileges at a hospital. They are responsible for determining what care is to be provided for their patient and coordinating the care. Physicians are the only professionals who may prescribe medication, or perform surgery or other intrusive treatments. They also do physical exams and work with patients who have health problems that arise from something being wrong with their bodies.

There are many specialties from which an aspiring physician may choose. Psychiatrists help people with psychological or emotional problems both by talking with them and through the prescription of psychotropic medications. Family practitioners provide comprehensive care to children and adults while focusing on both medical issues and the family as a whole. Surgeons provide medical care to patients needing to have something in their body removed, replaced, or repaired. Specialists in internal medicine (internists) have been trained to treat adults with a wide variety of illnesses. They must be excellent diagnosticians, know how the body works, and how illness and injury can change the body's functioning. Obstetricians provide care to pregnant women and deliver babies. Gynecologists specialize in disorders that affect women's reproductive systems. Physician's salaries may range from $100,000 to $300,000 depending on specialty, geographic region, hours worked, and work setting. Those employed by a health maintenance organization (HMO), VA medical center, or managed care program may receive a fixed salary. Those in private practice may work more hours, see more patients, and thus have higher earnings.

NURSES

Nursing plays a predominant role in the delivery of health care services to clients and their families in the types of agencies discussed in this chapter. The American Nursing Association (ANA) recognizes several levels of nursing practice, each level with its own requirements for education, training, and state licensure.

The Licensed Practical Nurse (LPN) requires one year of training which is offered by a vocational or technical school or community junior college. After completing the training, a state written exam is required before one can practice as an LPN. LPNs may distribute medication to patients, monitor vital signs, observe and assess daily functioning of a patient, and provide significant information to the client's treatment team. LPNs support and carry out the treatment plans made by the team; they may lead patient education or support groups under the supervision of a registered nurse.

LPNs and nursing assistants (NAs) spend the greatest amount of time with the patient and therefore are in a unique position to provide information to the treatment team when assessing the success of treatment interventions. Patients often find it easier to relate and talk to an LPN or NA, as they are often perceived as less authoritative and therefore less threatening psychologically to a patient.

A registered nurse (RN) completes either a two-year approved college program and receives an AD or AA (Associate Degree) in registered nursing, or a four-year college nursing program and graduates with a BSN (Bachelor of Science in Nursing). The ANA has made the BSN the standard for professional entry into nursing. Whichever way the RN is obtained, a state licensing exam is required to practice, and continuing education credits are required to retain the license.

The RN has many administrative functions on the ward level and needs good management and interpersonal skills. The RN is usually the team coordinator on an inpatient ward and is responsible for the activity and schedules of other nursing staff. He or she implements the multidisciplinary treatment plan for each patient; and coordinates the delivery of health care, from seeing that the patient gets the correct diet and receives other therapeutic treatments scheduled (x-ray, dental, occupational therapy, physical therapy, etc.) to assuring that the patient gets to appointments on time. An RN oversees the dispensing of medication by an LPN, sets the work schedules of other nursing staff, and insures that coverage at any given time is adequate to provide quality care. RNs provide patient education on health matters and information on preventive health management. Inpatient facilities, open 24 hours a day, afford all level of nursing staff the most opportunity to interact with patients, meet with their families, and have a significant effect on the patient's overall sense of well being.

The BSN-degreed nurse carries out all of the above functions and, because of additional education and training, provides a comprehensive level of knowledge-based practice. In preparation for a BSN, emphasis is placed on considerable course and lab work in the natural sciences--chemistry, biology, physiology, and math--as well as integrating course work in human development, and basic psychology. English and writing skills for documentation are essential.

The advanced level of nursing is the Masters in Nursing (MSN), also known as clinical nurse specialist, nurse practitioner, or nursing administrator. This degree provides the opportunity for advanced education in a specialty area such as geriatrics, pediatrics, mental health, surgery, oncology, or administration. These professionals operate with considerable independence and responsibility. They provide education for less well-trained nursing staff, do group and individual psychological therapy, work with patient's families, do discharge planning and follow up, conduct quality assurance reviews to ensure that hospital policies are effectively carried out, or provide leadership for hospital committees. The advanced degree requires an additional two years of college work and a placement for supervised experience in the area of one's specialty. State licensing exams are required before practice at the MSN level.

There is one other level of nursing-related careers that is important to the overall quality of and delivery of health care. People entering at this level are referred to as nursing assistants (NAs), certified nursing assistants (CNAs), mental health technicians (MHTs), or licensed mental health technicians (LMHTs), depending on where they work. NAs and MHTs require a high school degree or GED. These certified or licensed staff have received an additional 6-12 weeks of training at either a community college or vocational/technical school. On-the-job training is provided by the employing health care facility. People in these entry positions receive training about how to manage patients with medical and emotional limitations, how to lift and move them, how to read physician's orders, how to assist patients with basic care issues such as feeding themselves, bathing, dressing, and personal hygiene. NAs and MHTs escort patients to appointments and recreational activities, participate in small-group activities with patients, assist patients to conduct ward government, and are often called upon to assist in managing a patient who is exhibiting disruptive behavior.

Personal attributes for careers in nursing would include the abilities to work well with others, follow directions, and be able to set and keep personal boundaries (limit personal involvement) between themselves and patients. One should be able to communicate observations and patient assessments both verbally and in writing. For the student who is interested in pursing the four-year BSN degree, aptitudes for science and math, good leadership skills, and ability to direct others are desirable.

RNs may earn from $28,000 to $50,000. LPNs may earn from $18,400 to $27,000. Nursing assistants and MHTs salaries may range from $11,000 to $24,000, depending on education, experience, and work setting.

PHYSICAL THERAPISTS

Physical therapists work with patients to help improve their mobility, range of motion, relieve pain, or reduce the physical limitations that may result from illness or injury. Physical therapists see patients who have been referred to them with conditions such as a head injury, multiple sclerosis, chronic pain, fractures, amputations, or recovery from surgery or burns. They work with patients to help them achieve their highest level of functioning.

Treatment by a physical therapist may include stretching and flexibility exercises; massage; manipulation of stiff joints; use of ultrasound, heat, or cold to decrease pain and increase range of motion. People who become physical therapists must know anatomy, physiology, biology, and other science-related courses that apply to the functioning of the human body. The entry level for physical therapists is the bachelor's degree from an accredited program and successful completion of the licensing exam.

Physical therapists must be able to work with a variety of people, some who are in a great deal of physical pain and emotional distress. They must be able to assess the patient's abilities and design a treatment program that will expand those abilities, and must be able to write treatment plans and progress notes to keep other treatment team members informed about the patient's progress. Physical therapists must be able to use a variety of equipment, bend, stoop, lift, and stand for long periods of time. This career is very physically demanding. A salaried physical therapist may earn from $18,000 to $53,000. Many physical therapists also have private practices, and tend to earn more than the salaried workers.

OCCUPATIONAL THERAPISTS

Registered Occupational Therapists (OTRs) and Certified Occupational Therapy Assistants (COTAs) have an integral role on the treatment team. The OTR helps the patient return to their highest level of functioning and helps the patient to adapt to a more limited level if their disability is permanent.

In acute medical settings and rehabilitation hospitals, OTRs assess patients to determine their ability to perform normal activities of daily living: feeding themselves, dressing, bathing, understanding and communicating verbally and in writing. The OTR may design adaptive equipment for the patient's use, make splints to support or strengthen a weakened hand or arm, or work with the patients and their families to provide education about the prescribed rehabilitation program. The OTR may visit the patient's home to determine the need for adaptive equipment or advise about structural changes that can be made to accommodate the patient when he or she returns home.

In mental health facilities, long term care, and nursing homes, OTRs develop individual treatment plans for patients to help them maintain an interest in daily activities and improve their quality of life. In OT clinics, activities are designed to encourage socialization and interaction, and to encourage communication and lessen isolation. If depression, anxiety, or agitation is a part of the diagnosis, the OTR can recommend activities that can encourage expression of feelings through positive and creative means such as leather work, ceramics, wood working, and other nonverbal media. Often patients who are severely troubled can relate through activities such as painting or making a ceramic bowl much easier than they can talking to someone. These activities provide the OTR with another way to relate to and help the patient. Physical and creative activity programs can also be designed to divert focus from overwhelming problems or depression.

Residents in nursing homes often are there because they cannot adequately care for themselves at home. The OT can evaluate and design programs for patients to be involved in while assessing their strengths and difficulties in caring for themselves if they return home. The programs designed by OTRs can assist patients to maintain a quality of life close to what was enjoyed in an earlier time.

The Certified Occupational Therapy Assistant (COTA) works under the supervision of the OT. They often are the one who actually puts the devised OT plan into action, working directly with the patient. COTAs contribute their knowledge and skills in assessing patients, communicating and coordinating the OT program with other team members, and helping the patient find new ways to do things. The COTA works very closely with the patient, and can provide encouragement, enhancing the patient's sense of self worth and accomplishment. An important part of the health care field is helping patients regain their sense of capability and self worth.

Occupational therapy is a medically-oriented profession, not just a profession of working with arts and crafts. Their training and education requires a rigorous program, usually five years, to earn a bachelor's degree. As with other professions, there is a national accreditation body that approves college and university OT programs. Some states also require a license and continuing education credits to maintain the license.

If you are in high school and considering OT as a career choice, you should consider taking college preparatory courses in science, biology, and chemistry. A good grade point average in high school and the first two years of college (at least 3.5 prior to acceptance by the OT

Department), volunteer experience working with people with disabilities, ability to relate to people on an individual basis, and tolerance of individual differences are assets that would be helpful if considering a career as an OT or COTA. OTRs who are salaried average between $30,500 and $45,000. Beginning COTAs, who are generally paid an hourly rate, average between $8.50 and $15.00 per hour.

RECREATION THERAPISTS

Recreation therapists use activities--games, music, bowling, sports, or crafts--to help patients improve their self-esteem and functioning. They work with patients individually and in groups to help them socialize and increase their ability to be more independent and self-assured. Recreation therapists also work with people to improve general health, physical activity, and mental health.

Many recreation therapists work in inpatient or nursing home settings. They provide healthy opportunities for the patients to stay active and relate to others in the care facility. Recreation therapists may also work in the community, working at recreation centers, school special education programs, or programs for the elderly or the disabled.

Music therapists, one type of recreation therapist, work with patients to use music to express their feelings, to feel better about themselves, or to communicate better with others. Music therapists may work with people who have had extensive training in music or no musical experience at all. For example, while working with geriatric demented patients, music therapists use music activities to assist them to become a member of a group, to follow instructions, and to feel a sense of self worth. Music therapy, like other recreational therapy modalities, offers a wide range of activities so that almost all patients may participate. The average salary of a recreation therapist was $25,557 in 1991. In the Federal Government, the average for all recreational therapists was about $33,500.

ADDITIONAL INFORMATION AND RESOURCES

American Association of Colleges of Nursing
American Counseling Association
American Health Care Association

American Medical Association
American Nursing Association
American Occupational Therapy Association
American Psychological Association
American Rehabilitation Counselors Association
Association for Drug and Alcohol Counselors
National Association for Practical Nurse Education and Service
National Association of Social Work
National League for Nursing
Occupational Therapy Association
Physical Therapy Association

Additional references in this field can be found in the following:

National Association of Social Workers (ND). *Choices: Careers in Social Work.* [Pamphlet]. Washington, DC: National Association of Social Workers.
Palmisano, J., (Ed.) (1993). *Mental health and social work career directory.* Detroit, MI: Gale Research, Inc.

Chapter 9

CAREERS IN RESIDENTIAL TREATMENT AND COMMUNITY-BASED SUPPORT PROGRAMS

Ruth Torkelson Lynch
Ross K. Lynch

Federal policy, funding, and philosophical changes that emphasize support for people with disabilities have resulted in dramatic modifications in how and where services are provided. Since service delivery expectations and settings have changed, helping profession careers have also changed. Career opportunities have expanded within residential and community-based support programs.

Since the late 1960s, there has been a dramatic shift in how rehabilitation services are provided to individuals who need comprehensive, long-term residential treatment and support. Direct service responsibilities and funding have been transferred from large, self-contained state residential institutions to small privately owned, residential facilities operating in the community. As a result, many individuals with chronic conditions such as mental illness or developmental disabilities have moved from large institutional settings to smaller community-based settings. Residential services often involve life-long support and supervision.

There has also been increased demand for alternative residential treatment and transitional options to meet the needs of individuals with other health concerns (e.g., alcohol and other drug abuse, emotional disorders, dual diagnosis, eating disorders, brain injury) as they progress from inpatient care to outpatient treatment to independence. This trend has created a need for residential-based services that are a transition between hospitalization and home. Transitional living centers, also referred to as community re-entry programs, are designed for medically stable individuals with good potential for independent living but who have problems (e.g., cognitive, emotional, behavioral) that are not well managed in the community on an outpatient basis.

Admission to transitional programs may be from acute care medical or rehabilitation settings or directly from the community. Financial reimbursement patterns (e.g., conversion of inpatient mental health benefits to outpatient benefits) and managed care (e.g., intensive case management, needs assessments and planning) have been stimulants for this growth of residential treatment programs in the community. Philosophical, economic, and public policy shifts that emphasize client independence and also provide services in the least restrictive and least expensive environment have led to a rapid rise in community-living and community-based residential treatment options. Residential care models provide 24-hour-, 7-days-per-week care, supervision, or both. They differ substantially in terms of size, cost, staffing, program structure, and content. Changes in program models have had great impact on the career opportunities, demands, and challenges for individuals who work in residential settings.

PROGRAM MODELS

Residential treatment and community-based support services include supported independent living, specialized foster homes, group homes, integrated and clustered apartments, and free-standing residential facilities. An overview of program models is presented to orient individuals considering careers in residential settings.

The Commission on Accreditation of Rehabilitation Facilities (CARF) (CARF, 1994) and the Joint Commission on Accreditation of Healthcare Organizations (JCAHO) (JCAHO, 1994) are two accrediting bodies that develop and maintain program standards, organizational plans, and personnel guidelines related to residential treatment and community-based support programs. Terminology from the *1994 Standards Manual and Interpretive Guidelines for Organizations Serving People with Disabilities* (CARF, 1994) has been used in the examples of residential programs.

Community-Integrated Residential Programs for Individuals with Brain Injury

The number of individuals with severe brain injuries who survive their initial injuries but require long-term (perhaps life-long) services has increased dramatically in recent years. Community-integrated programs for individuals with brain injury assist them to accomplish the functional outcomes of home and community integration and engage in productive activities (CARF, 1994). These services are frequently provided as a transition from initial intensive medical care and inpatient medical rehabilitation to community-living. Since individuals with brain injury have such varying functional needs and may continue to make functional gains over time, residential programs for individuals with brain injury range from highly-structured residences to community-living support programs.

Community-Living Programs

Integrated living programs are offered in homes or apartments and may include supervised living, supported independent living, and family living. Supervised living is a program that provides individualized care, supervision, support, and training to maintain and promote self-sufficiency. This type of service may involve assistance at night or at other times when the person served is at home. Supported independent living provides support to persons who are primarily independent, but who need some assistance (e.g., with personal care) that enables them to have maximum self direction and maintain their independence. Staff are available as needed or on a planned, periodic basis to offer assistance, but not supervision, in an individual's home. Family living programs provide a family environment through a contractual relationship in the home of a family. Individuals with disabilities participate as family members and a community agency provides support and monitoring for the living arrangements.

Congregate living programs provide residential services in large communal living arrangements that are basically self-sustaining and may be clustered in a setting similar to a campus. Such programs provide individualized care, supervision, support, and training to maintain and promote self-sufficiency. Personnel are present at night and at other times when the persons being served are at home.

Residential Treatment Programs for Individuals with Alcohol and/or Other Drug Problems

These programs provide a temporary living environment where persons with Alcohol and/or Other Drug (AOD) problems receive supervision, support, and treatment from personnel who are available 24 hours a day. The goal is to provide knowledge and resources to allow participants to end their involvement with alcohol and other drugs.

Residential Mental Health Treatment Programs

Mental health residential programs are staffed to provide general and specialized interdisciplinary services 24 hours per day for persons with psychiatric disabilities whose acute symptomatology has been stabilized, although not resolved. These individuals have persistent dysfunction in several major life areas to an extent which requires a total therapeutically-planned environment for group living and learning.

Community Support Programs

The Community Support Program (CSP) framework permits persons with psychiatric disabilities access to a network of agencies and professional providers that can flexibly provide services in the community. With direction from the National Institute on Mental Health (1989), community service networks are organized around a coordinating agency that has primary responsibility for developing the system of care and assuring continuity of treatment. This model of service provides a full range of services: housing alternatives, crisis and outreach services, vocational rehabilitation, peer support programs, case management, skill training, and integrated rehabilitation programs. The most effective CSPs emphasize a dual focus: skill building for community life and supportive environments.

CAREER OPPORTUNITIES IN RESIDENTIAL AND COMMUNITY-SUPPORT

The staff of residential and community-based support programs are typically comprised of direct care staff and professional/managerial staff. While the job duties and expectations for these staff differ on some levels, there are also common features associated with employment in these settings. Direct care staff have the following responsibilities: participate on a team; provide a safe and clean environment; manage activities of daily living; maintain client health; organize leisure and recreational activities; and maintain the operations of the program. Managers and professional staff should have good interpersonal work skills, the ability to teach, and the ability to develop programming which enhances normalization in the community.

Direct-Care Staff

Direct-care staff, also referred to as attendants, aides, client care workers, or primary care providers, comprise a large percentage of personnel in residential facilities and support programs. Direct care staff teach and are involved in active habilitative treatment in addition to supervising clients. Therapy conducted as part of the day-to-day residential activities is critical to client improvement and is often more effective than that conducted in formal therapy sessions (Durrant, 1993). Due to the very intense daily interactions and influence which direct-care staff have with clients, residential facilities will always be highly dependent on the quality and performance of direct-care staff.

Human services worker is a generic term utilized by the U.S. Department of Labor (*Occupational Outlook Handbook*, 1994) for workers with various job titles related to direct care. A strong desire to help others, patience, understanding, good communication skills, a strong sense of responsibility, and effective time management are valued personal characteristics. These individuals play important roles in community settings, providing daily supervision and support, teaching independent living skills, providing emotional support, and leading recreational activities. While some employment is available for high school graduates, most employers prefer applicants with some college preparation in human services, social work, or one of the social or behavioral sciences (e.g., rehabilitation, special education, sociology). Certificate and associate degree programs in human services or mental health are offered at community and junior colleges or vocational-technical institutes. Formal education is almost always necessary for advancement.

The job outlook for human services workers is expected to double between 1992 and 2005 making it among the most rapidly growing occupations. Residential setting expansion will contribute to growth. Starting salaries for human service workers range from about $12,000 to $20,000 per year with experienced workers generally earning between $15,000 and $25,000 annually.

Psychiatric aides and psychiatric technicians, also referred to as mental health assistants or psychiatric nursing assistants, may work in residential care facilities such as halfway houses, private psychiatric facilities, and community mental health centers. Psychiatric technicians participate in rehabilitation and treatment programs by providing direct care, personal hygiene assistance, and supervision for individuals with mental illness, emotional disorders, or mental retardation. In many instances, neither a high school diploma nor previous work experience is necessary but opportunities for advancement require formal training. Excluding high and low salary groups, the middle 50% of nursing and psychiatric aides earn between $11,000 and $18,000.

Professional Staff

A wide array of professionals function within residential treatment and community support programs. These professionals must work as a team, listening to each other in a nonjudgemental fashion, seeing their decisions as group rather than individual decisions, and actively participating in making decisions with the client.

Counselors, particularly rehabilitation counselors and mental health counselors, are employed in residential and community-based support programs. Rehabilitation counselors help persons deal with the personal, social, and vocational impact of disability. Mental health counselors help individuals deal with addictions and substance abuse; family, parenting, and marital problems; stress management; and other issues of mental and emotional health. Generally, counselors have a master's degree in counseling or a related field. Counselors may hold positions in residential settings as behavioral specialists, personal adjustment counselors, vocational specialists, or case managers.

Employment for counselors is expected to grow faster than the average for all occupations with particularly strong demand for rehabilitation and mental health counselors. Salaries in the middle range are typically $24,000 to $41,500.

Occupational therapists help individuals with mentally, physically, developmentally, or emotionally disabling conditions to develop, recover, or maintain daily living and work skills. Intervention focuses on improvement of basic motor functions and reasoning abilities as well as accommodations for permanent loss of function. Occupational therapists in residential and community-based support programs focus on daily living skills, time management skills, budgeting, shopping, homemaking, and use of public transportation. A bachelor's degree in occupational therapy is the minimal requirement for entry into this field. The majority of states require a license to practice occupational therapy which requires a degree plus a passing score on a national certification examination.

Employment is expected to increase much faster than average due to anticipated growth in demand for rehabilitation and long-term care services. Salaries typically range from $30,500 to $45,000.

Psychologists study human behavior and mental processes to understand, explain, and change people's behavior. Psychologists may serve as consultants to residential and support programs or as staff members. A doctoral degree and attainment of licensure (through appropriate education, internship, and professional experience) are generally required for practicing psychologists. Salaries for psychologists vary widely depending on specific psychological training (e.g., clinical, counseling, school) and work setting. As an example, $54,400 is the average salary for psychologists in the Federal government.

Recreational therapists, also referred to as activity directors or therapeutic recreation specialists, employ activities to treat or maintain the physical, mental, and emotional well being of patients. Activities include sports, games, dance, drama, arts and crafts, music, and community field trips. In residential facilities, group-oriented activities are emphasized. Community-based recreational therapists work in park and recreation departments helping individuals develop leisure activities and provide them with opportunities for exercise, mental stimulation, creativity, and fun.

Educational preparation options include a bachelor's degree in therapeutic recreation; an associate degree in recreational therapy; or training in art, drama, or music therapy. Recreational therapist salaries vary depending on work setting, job demands, and educational preparation but generally average between $20,000 and $26,000.

Registered nurses develop and manage nursing care plans; observe, assess, and record symptoms, reactions, and progress; administer and monitor medications; instruct individuals how to improve and maintain their health; and consult with the treatment team regarding health issues. To obtain a nursing license, all states require graduation from an accredited nursing school and passing a national licensing examination. There are three major educational preparation paths: an Associate Degree (ADN) nursing diploma from a two-year community or junior college program; a Bachelor of Science degree in Nursing (BSN) from a 4- to 5-year college or university program; or a 2- to 3-year diploma program from a hospital. Individuals considering nursing should realize that advancement opportunities are broader for those with a BSN. and some career paths are open only to nurses with bachelor's or advanced degrees. Nursing education includes classroom instruction and supervised training in hospitals and other health facilities.

Nurses must be able to accept responsibility, direct or supervise others, follow orders precisely, and determine when consultation is required. Employment for nurses is expected to grow much faster than average for all occupations with particularly high growth in home health care and related services that allow individuals to be in a transitional or home setting. Salaries for RNs vary with work setting and level of responsibility, ranging from $22,000 to $50,000 with a median salary of $34,000.

Social workers provide individual and group therapy, outreach, crisis intervention, and facilitate family involvement. The social worker in a residential treatment setting may have primary responsibility for planning discharge or coordinating transition from one program to another. A bachelor's degree satisfies the minimum requirement for some positions, especially small community agencies, and can be acquired through undergraduate majors in related fields (e.g., psychology, sociology) or social work (BSW). An MSW degree, generally required for positions in health and mental health settings, prepares graduates to perform assessment, to manage cases, and to supervise other workers. Master's degree programs usually last two years and include supervised field instruction. Social work practice and titles are regulated by state licensing, certification, or registration laws. Employment of social workers is expected to increase faster than the average for all occupations. The median earnings of MSW social workers is about $30,000.

Speech language pathologists treat persons with speech, language, voice and fluency disorders. They counsel individuals and their families about communication disorders; work with family members to recognize and change behavior patterns that impede communication; and work with clients and treatment staff to implement communication-enhancing techniques into the home or residence. Speech-language pathologists are particularly involved in residential and community-support programs for individuals with strokes or brain injury who experience communication problems. A master's degree in speech-language pathology is the standard credential for the field. Most states have licensing laws that require a master's degree; supervised clinical experience; a passing score on a national examination; and post-graduate professional experience. Employment of speech-language pathologists is expected to increase much faster than the average for all occupations. The middle salaries range between $27,500 and $42,000.

SUMMARY

There are common characteristics of employees in residential treatment and community-based support programs regardless of job title or professional preparation. It is important for persons in these settings to have a philosophical belief that residential and community-based support are reasonable and valuable resources for individuals who require long-term and/or transitional services. The ability to communicate and work cooperatively with other professionals is also important because residential treatment models rely on interdisciplinary professional input through a team approach. Community treatment is most effective if each staff member recognizes that all interactions and daily activities (e.g., working cooperatively on a chore, eating a meal) have therapeutic potential and are learning or treatment opportunities. For professionals who wish to develop treatment plans and be present in daily living settings to implement them, residential treatment and community-support programs offer potentially satisfying career opportunities.

Although it can be very rewarding to provide practical assistance to individuals who are becoming independent, the responsibility of 24-hours-per-day supervision of persons with complex and often life-long needs can create great personal strain. One must understand personal and professional demands of careers in residential treatment and implement steps to manage the challenges and stressors. Individuals seeking careers in these settings should be able to deal with difficult emotional situations; be cohesive and supportive of other team members; be personally integrated (i.e., clear-headed, stable, with a positive sense of self); and possess "psychic energy, enthusiasm, and optimism, all couched within a realistic framework" (Miskimins, 1990, p. 881). Clearly, there are great opportunities to find a rewarding and challenging career helping people to attain their maximum potential in home and community.

ADDITIONAL INFORMATION AND RESOURCES

Additional information regarding these careers is available from counselors and career centers. You might refer to the most recent edition of the *Occupational Outlook Handbook* or you could contact the professional associations below. The addresses are found in Appendix A.

>   American Counseling Association
>   American Health Care Association
>   American Nurses' Association; National League for Nursing
>   American Occupational Therapy Association
>   American Psychological Association
>   American Speech, Language, and Hearing Association
>   American Therapeutic Recreation Association
>   Council for Standards in Human Service Education
>   National Association of Social Workers
>   National Council on Therapeutic Recreation
>   National Organization for Human Services Education

Additional information can be found in the following:

Commission on Accreditation of Rehabilitation Facilities. (1994). *1994 Standards Manual and Interpretive Guidelines for Organizations Serving People with Disabilities.* Tucson, Arizona: Author.

Durrant, M. (1993). *Residential treatment: A cooperative, competency-based approach to therapy and program design.* New York: W. W. Norton.

Joint Commission on Accreditation of Healthcare Organizations (1995). *Comprehensive accreditation manual for hospitals.* Chicago, IL: Author.

Joint Commission on Accreditation of Healthcare Organizations. (1988). *1989 Consolidated Standards Manual (Mental Health, Substance Abuse, MR/DD Standards).* Chicago: Author.

Miskimins, R. W. (1990). A theoretical model for the practice of residential treatment. *Adolescence, 25*(100), 867-890.

National Institute of Mental Health (1989). *Toward a model plan for a comprehensive community-based mental health system.* Rockville, MD: U.S. Department of Health and Human Services; Alcohol, Drug, and Mental Health Administration.

U. S. Department of Labor. (1994). *Occupational Outlook Handbook.* Washington, D. C.: Author.

Chapter 10

ACCREDITATION AND CREDENTIALING

Dennis W. Engels
Beth Durodoye
Carolyn Kern

How do you find a competent counselor or mental health provider? How do you distinguish one counselor from another? Seeking information about a professional's educational background and credentials is one way to start the process of identifying qualified mental health professionals. Students considering a program of study can learn much by knowing that a program is or is not accredited. Clients can have assurance that graduates of accredited programs have completed a preparation program that meets or exceeds national standards. This chapter presents information about two major aspects of quality control in mental health professions--accreditation of preparation programs and credentialing of providers. The terms "accreditation" and "credentialing" are often confused: preparation programs are accredited; individual professionals are credentialed (e.g., they have a license or a certificate).

Accreditation of preparation programs implies a high level of quality determined from a thorough review process. An individual's credential--a state or national certificate or a state license--requires that a mental health practitioner complete an extensive academic preparation program with supervised practica and internship experiences. This education and supervised experience is followed by a comprehensive application and assessment process.

The first part of this chapter will focus on accreditation of mental health preparation programs. It will be followed by sections on certification and licensure, a discussion of related issues, and a brief conclusion.

Mental health professionals have the responsibility of upholding and maintaining credibility within and outside the profession. This responsibility is ongoing and emphasizes accreditation and credentialing, ethics, and education. Accreditation and credentialing act as ways to validate the profession while providing maximum protection of the public. Credentialed providers are required to adhere to ethical standards. Ethical standards serve as guidelines for acceptable practice in the profession and provide a means by which the profession may monitor itself. Formal education in mental health preparation programs acts as an introduction to the profession and serves to increase professional awareness, knowledge, and skills. Continuing education takes place when mental health providers join professional associations, attend seminars and workshops, and read relevant literature. Through activities such as these, mental health professionals maintain the professional quality of their fields.

PROFESSIONAL ASSOCIATIONS

Readers will find many different professional associations listed in the Appendix of this book. These associations are organizations of professionals and, sometimes, paraprofessionals and students, who share common goals and interests and who work to promote those goals and their profession. Newsletters, journals, conferences, and other meetings are means for exchanging ideas, promoting members' professional development, and promoting the profession. Good professional mental health organizations also promote the mental health of the general public. Readers can obtain information about any of these associations by writing to the addresses listed in the Appendix.

ACCREDITATION

Accreditation is the most generally recognized assurance that a professional education program meets highly exacting standards in its organization, faculty and staff, core curriculum, and clinical preparation. While accreditation is available for both institutions and specific programs within institutions, discussion here is focused on accreditation for preparation programs. Accreditation assures the public, especially prospective students, that programs meet high standards. Accreditation also promotes improvement of academic programs. By promoting high standards and on-going program refinements, accreditation is a means of self regulation and refinement within a profession and is an incentive for non-accredited programs to meet the standards associated with accredited programs.

Hospitals and residential care centers are accredited by the Joint Commission on Health Care Organizations (JCAHO). JCAHO reviewers assess the quality of patient care and coordination of services provided--e.g., medical, psychological, social, rehabilitative. This accreditation body also conducts both scheduled and unscheduled accreditation visits to assure quality patient care.

Accreditation of academic preparation programs--such as in mental health preparation--is a bit different. The accreditation process assists faculty members to interact in very focused ways, all with the aim of meeting or exceeding established and recognized standards of the profession. Accreditation is very demanding, and potentially very rewarding. Intensive self examination by program faculty, staff, and students, and periodic external evaluation of programs by accreditation experts in a profession can be a major force for program improvement. For example, faculty, students, staff, and others connected with a preparation program conduct formal and informal discussions and examinations of program admission standards and procedures, curriculum content, course sequence, campus and off-campus clinical counseling and supervision standards. They also obtain evaluations from current and former students and employers. Accreditation requirements for intensive collaboration, examination, and discussion by all members of the educational team can have tremendous positive effects in the form of staff, faculty, and program refinement; verification of strengths; recognition of areas needing improvement; and overall personnel and program renewal. All these are combined in a written document called a "self study" which may provide significant opportunities for insight and program improvement

The visiting team has responsibilities for examining and helping to refine the program. The visiting team examines the self study and conducts the site visit. Following the visit, the visiting team completes its report and submits it to the accrediting board which makes a final decision about the quality of the preparation program. The school is then informed of their accreditation status--for example, is the program approved for accreditation, is it on probation with deficiencies to be corrected, or does it not meet the standards and therefore is not accredited. The accreditation status is made public in newsletters and journals. Accredited schools often include this status in descriptive materials about their program.

Accreditation provides quality assurance for the students, the public, the institution, and the profession. In some professional specialties, students who complete accredited programs can sit for credentialing examinations at the time of graduation or before, while graduates of other programs may have to meet additional criteria before licensing or credentialing.

Professional preparation standards are promoted and influenced by organizations such as the American Counseling Association (ACA), the American Association for Marriage and Family Therapy (AAMFT), the American Association for Pastoral Counselors (AAPC), the American Psychological Association (APA) the American Rehabilitation Counseling Association (ARCA), the American Medical Association (AMA), the National Association of Social Workers (NASW), and others. Each of these associations promotes accreditation and is affiliated with an accreditation body. Specific information about these accrediting bodies and their specific accreditation processes can be obtained from the appropriate professional association or the accrediting body [addresses are listed in the Appendix]. Students considering admission to a mental health preparation program should investigate the accreditation status of the programs they are considering as one important criterion for program selection. Accredited programs have rigorous admission standards and somewhat lengthy application procedures; so students would be advised to begin their search as early as possible. An excellent question to ask about any preparation program is, "Are you accredited, and by what accrediting agencies"? Follow the answer you get by reading about that accreditation and ask how the accreditation assists graduates in obtaining a license or other credential.

PROFESSIONAL CREDENTIALING

Credentialing encompasses two primary methods mental health professionals use to demonstrate their credibility to the public. A certificate or a license is the "credentialing mechanism" of the profession (Brooks and Gerstein, 1990). A license is granted based on laws passed at the state level. Gerstein and Brooks (1990) have said that legislation helps define counselor roles, legalize counselor practice, and protect consumers from incompetent practitioners. Certificates are credentials awarded by associations or organizations that verify that the professional has met certain requirements defined by a professional organization or association. The following discussion will focus on certification before proceeding to licensure.

Certification

National certification is one form of mental health credentialing that counselors may obtain within their professions. Certification is a process by which professional recognition is granted to practitioners who adhere to guidelines established by specific certification bodies. Certifications on a national level are voluntary and may be granted by agencies, governmental organizations, or associations. State level certificates are regulated according to state laws or policies. For some counseling occupations, participation in the state certification process is mandatory, as exemplified by state requirements of certification for school counselors as a prerequisite for employment. Certification occurs at both the national and state levels.

The National Board for Certified Counselors (NBCC) is the largest general practice and specialty counselor certification body. NBCC certification is based on the premise that all counselors work from a knowledge base that is standard for the profession (Sweeney, 1991). NBCC is an independent corporation which (a) maintains a national certification system, (b) provides public and peer recognition for certified counselors, and (c) maintains an index of all certified counselors (NBCC, 1992; Stone, 1985).

Other specialty certifications are granted to qualified counselors through NBCC. Specialties include certification in career counseling--National Certified Career Counselor (NCCC); mental health counseling--Certified Clinical Mental Health Counselor (CCMHC); school counseling--National Certified School Counselor (NCSC); gerontological counseling--National Certified Gerontological Counselor (NCGC), and addictions counseling--Master Addictions Counselor (MAC).

Counselors and other mental health professionals may also obtain specialty certifications that are independent from NBCC (Forrest and Stone, 1991). For example, rehabilitation counselors are granted a specialty certificate by the Commission on Rehabilitation Counselor

Certification as a Certified Rehabilitation Counselor (CRC), and the International Association for Marriage and Family Therapy grants a credential to marriage and family therapists--Licensed Marriage and Family Therapist (LMFT).

NBCC highlights several features that distinguish national certification from state licensure. Certification is broad in scope and offers national networking and referral opportunities. The certification process is guided by the counseling profession, whereas licensure is a matter of state law. While certification recognizes specialty areas, most state licenses do not. Finally, certification recognizes competencies, but is not authorization to practice, while licensure authorizes the provider to practice.

Licensure

Licensure is a legal status granted to individuals by the state in which they provide professional services. Psychologists, physicians, professional counselors, lawyers, nurses, social workers, and many other professionals must be licensed to practice in their state. Requirements for licensure vary by specialty and by state. In most states, in order to practice or represent yourself as a professional--e.g., counselor, psychologist, or social worker--you must be licensed in that state.

Some states have a title act and others have a practice act. A title act restricts use of the title of the particular professional--e.g., *licensed professional counselor*--to those who are licensed. A practice act restricts the activity of counseling to those who are licensed.

Some states require licensure only for those who are in private practice. Mental health professionals working in institutional settings (such as schools & universities, mental health centers, churches, hospitals, etc.) may be exempt from state licensure requirements. While most states have similar requirements for licensure, aspiring professionals should communicate directly with the licensing board in a specific state to obtain license information. In our changing world, it is important to keep employment options as broad as possible. Since most states have passed licensure laws, one should seriously consider those licensure requirements when choosing a graduate preparation program.

The minimum requirement for licensure as a counselor or social worker is a master's degree from a regionally accredited university. Additional requirements may include supervised experience, written examination, and letters of reference. Licensure as a psychologist requires a doctorate in most states. Specific course work, supervised experience, and passing an examination are additional requirements. The supervisor of internship experiences--either pre- or post-degree experience--may have to have specific credentials in order for the applicant to eventually obtain licensing. Some states, for example, require that supervisors have special training and credentials in supervision before their supervisees can be licensed. Questions about supervisor credentials need to be answered by the licensing board in each state or by the certification body that the applicant is interested in. Organizations that can help you get information about current regulations are listed in the Appendix.

Purpose of Licensure

Licensure was established to protect the public and the public's right to choose providers. Licensure also enhances the credibility of the profession. By ensuring that professional providers meet all legal requirements, a licensing body can protect the public. Generally, a state legislature regulates the practice of the profession through a board whose members are appointed by the governor of the state.

Licensure provides standardization within a state allowing insurance companies a basis for issuing payments to licensed professionals. Most health insurance companies will not make payments (called "third-party payment") to professionals unless they are licensed by an approved state professional licensing board.

Licensure, which is granted by state law, provides a number of protections for the consumer and the practitioner. It assures the public that those who practice as licensed professionals have met a minimum standard of education and training. Licensed professionals have achieved a level of competency required to provide services. Licensure often provides a legal assurance of privileged communication for the client who reveals information in a therapeutic setting (e.g., counseling session). A licensed professional is more likely to be reimbursed by third-party payers for their services. Licensure, however, is not a guarantee of competence.

Requirements for Maintaining Licensure

Once a mental health professional obtains a license, they must complete continuing education credits as a way to help them stay current in their field. Each state has specific conditions that must be met in order to maintain a license in that state. Additionally, states require a license maintenance fee. Continuing education hours may be obtained by additional course work in an approved area at a college or university, or, more often, licensed professionals attend board sanctioned workshops and professional meetings that have various seminars related to the mental health profession and the professional's current needs.

SOME FINAL THOUGHTS

Preparing to enter a mental health profession can be the start or continuation of a life-long journey of personal and professional growth, research, and service to others. Because our world changes so rapidly and so profoundly, no education is ever completely finished. Mental health education programs and degrees provide a sound preparation and foundation for a lifetime of challenging and rewarding professionalism.

Accreditation, certification, and licensure are all vitally important to mental health professionals. Readers interested in a counseling or human services profession should seek accreditation information about the programs that seem most interesting and appealing to them. Program representatives should also be able to provide information about how the program relates to certification and licensure standards. Wise selection of a program is a vitally important first step in developing the knowledge and skills needed for obtaining credentials and providing mental health services.

ADDITIONAL INFORMATION AND RESOURCES

The following associations all relate to accreditation or credentialing processes:

Academy of Certified Clinical Mental Health Counselors
American Association for Marriage and Family Therapy

American Association for Marriage and Family Therapy
American Medical Association
American Nursing Association
American Occupational Therapy Certification Board
American Psychological Association
Association of Social Work Boards
Commission on Accreditation of Rehabilitation Facilities
Commission of Rehabilitation Counselor Certification
Council for Accreditation of Counseling and Related Educational
    Programs
Joint Commission on Accreditation of Healthcare Organizations
National Association of Social Work
National Board for Certified Counselors
National Council on Therapeutic Recreation

The following sources provide good information on many topics discussed in this chapter:

Alberding, B., Lauver, P., & Patnoe, J. (1993). Counselor awareness of the consequences of certification and licensure. *Journal of Counseling and Development, 72*, 33-38.

Brooks, D.K., Jr., & Gerstein, L.H. (1990). Counselor credentialing and interprofessional collaboration. *Journal of Counseling and Development, 68*, 477-484.

Davis, T., Witmer, J., & Navin, S. (1990). Assessing the impact of counselor licensure in Ohio as perceived by counselors. *Counselor Education and Supervision, 30*, 37-47.

Forrest, D.V., & Stone, L.A. (1991). Counselor certification. In F.O. Bradley (Ed.), *Credentialing in counseling* (pp. 13-21). Alexandria, VA: American Association for Counseling and Development.

Gerstein, L.H., & Brooks, D.K. Jr. (1990). The helping profession's challenge: Credentialing and interdisciplinary collaboration. *Journal of Counseling and Development, 68*, 475-476.

Hollis, J.W., & Wantz, R.A. (1993). *Counselor preparation: 1993-1995, Volumes I(Programs and personnel) and II (Status, trends and implications), (8th ed)*. Muncie, IN: Accelerated Development.

NBCC: A guide to understanding counselor credentialing. (1992). National Board of Certified Counselors. [Brochure]. Greensboro, NC: Author.

Stone, L.A. (1985). National board for certified counselors: History, relationships, and projections. *Journal of Counseling and Development, 63,* 605-606.

Sweeney, T.J. (1991). Counselor credentialing: Purpose and origin. In F.O. Bradley (Ed.), *Credentialing in Counseling* (pp.1-12). Alexandria, VA: American Association of Counseling and Development.

Vacc, N.A., & Loesch, L.C. (1987). *Counseling as a profession.* Muncie, IN: Accelerated Development.

Chapter 11

WHAT NEXT?

Nancy J. Garfield
Brooke B. Collison

As you have read through this book you have learned much about counseling and human services careers and the career search process. You began by learning about the general characteristics or qualities of people who work in the helping professions and what types of educational programs and requirements there are for the counseling and human services fields. You then had the opportunity to explore seven different work settings where counselors and human services specialists work. You learned of professional opportunities that exist for people who wish to work with and help people. You also learned about credentialing and accreditation--the importance of accreditation of academic departments and training programs, and about the value of being a credentialed provider in those fields that encourage or require credentialing.

After all that reading, you may still be unsure about a specific occupational choice. This is a good time to review the check list you completed in Chapter 2. You may wish to use this information to talk with a counselor about occupations you are considering.

Talking with a counselor can provide you with an opportunity to learn more about yourself and your interests. You and your counselor may want to consider whether you could learn more about yourself by taking an interest inventory. Interest inventories are multiple choice assessment instruments that compare your likes and dislikes to those of people in a variety of different occupations. People with similar interests usually enjoy and succeed at the same types of occupations. Although interest inventories do not include all the occupations that have been discussed in this book, a number of them are included. Talk with a counselor about your likes and dislikes and what you are good at doing. Do you like to talk with people? listen to people? solve problems? or work with your hands to make or fix things? and how much school are you willing to attend? You also need to consider what subjects you do best in academically.

Making an occupational choice also involves learning about what is important to you. Discuss what type of work you like. Would you enjoy working regular hours? days? nights? Do you like a job where you can wear casual clothes such as blue jeans or would you prefer a job where you had to wear dressy clothes like a suit or dress most of the time? How much money do you think you will need to live in the style you would like?

If you think that one or more of the areas or occupations described in this book would interest you, there are several things that you could do: you could read the materials referenced in the chapter or chapters about your career choice; you could write to one of the professional associations listed in the Appendix; you could also talk with people who are working in those occupations. Find out what they do during their work week. How much time do they spend working with clients, doing paper work or report writing, consulting with others about their clients, or doing other tasks. Ask them what they like best and least about their jobs. Find out what they think is the future of their profession, what they think people in their field will be doing in 10 or 20 years. Ask to spend some time with them acting as a shadow to see what they do (this may not be possible in the confidential or private nature of many counseling and human services jobs). There are many tasks which you could experience to provide you with a better sense of the field, and would help you know if you want to join the profession.

Another way you can learn more about the helping professions is to find summer or part-time work in a field related to your interests. This experience will help you decide if your expressed occupational choice will be a good one for you, one which you will enjoy, find satisfying, and also provide you with the personal and financial rewards that are important to you. Within most schools are opportunities to work as an aide in a guidance office or a career center, as a tutor, or as a peer helper.

So what do you do now that you have all this information? Part of that decision depends on where you are in your academic program or career. If you are a high school student or just beginning your college program, select a field or major that will afford you the opportunity to get a good liberal arts education. It should include English composition, to enable you to write clearly and well for the reports you will need to complete; a solid grounding in mathematics; and courses in psychology and sociology, to help you begin to understand people. For the most part, you will need to have training beyond a bachelor's degree to work in the fields discussed earlier in the book.

Some careers require special undergraduate majors. School counseling [See Chapter 3] is an example. Most states require school counselors to have been certified and experienced as teachers before they can be school counselors. If you are thinking about a professional career which has specific educational major requirements at the undergraduate level, check those out before you move too far in a different academic major.

If you have completed your undergraduate degree, you will need to choose a graduate degree program that will enable you to do the type of work you have identified as your career choice. When you decide which work setting and which occupation you wish to pursue, then you will need to select a graduate school and course of study that will enable you to enter that profession. As you have read, many occupations require a master's degree, others will require a doctorate (PhD, PsyD, or EdD). You will need to ascertain what type of degree will be required for your occupational choice. Talk to people already in that profession, faculty at schools you are considering, and the state agencies that license or certify the profession you have chosen. Get information from the professional organizations of your career choice about what the minimum educational requirements and credentialing are for that occupation.

APPLYING TO GRADUATE PROGRAMS

Students generally need a 2.7 to a 3.0 minimum undergraduate grade point average, and at least the 50th percentile on a standardized test such as the Graduate Record Exam (GRE) or Miller's Analogies Test (MAT) for graduate school admission. Provisional admission may be possible if a student does not meet these standard requirements but can demonstrate other talents and strengths. Requirements vary in different graduate programs. Graduate applications usually need to be made by February or March for Fall enrollment and to seek graduate assistantships to work on campus. Many programs require a personal interview. Interested students should write both the graduate school to obtain an application and catalog and the program of interest to obtain curriculum guides, brochures, or assistantship information. Each program usually has a faculty admission committee and you may want to call or visit to learn more about the program. Sometimes more information on specific areas of graduate study can be obtained from professional associations. For example, the American College Personnel Association publishes entrance requirements for many graduate programs (See Kiem & Graham, 1994, in the reference list for Chapter 4).

Graduate assistantships are often available for students enrolled in professional study. Graduate assistants usually work 10 to 20 hours per week to earn a modest income and usually are provided a tuition waiver for graduate credits. On most campuses prospective students apply for graduate assistantships like any job. Assistantships are meaningful related work experiences in such areas as residence life or academic advising.

These are all topics to discuss with a counselor. Making a career choice is a process that involves learning about yourself and about the work world. Making a choice is a process that takes time. You must learn about what is important to you: what your values, your personal priorities, and your abilities are, and what personality characteristics you have that would or would not fit the occupations you are considering.

The next step is yours--it could be a big one. Good wishes.

Appendix A

ORGANIZATIONS AND ASSOCIATIONS

Names and addresses of the following associations or councils are included for your use. Addresses listed are the best addresses listed at the time this book was printed.

American Art Therapy Association
1202 Allanson Road
Mundelein, IL 66660

American Association for Adult and Continuing Education
1101 Connecticut Avenue, NW, Suite 700
Washington, DC 20036

American Association for Marriage and Family Therapy
1100 17th Street, NW
Washington, DC 20036

American Association for Music Therapy
P. O. Box 80012
Valley Forge, PA 19484

American Association of Colleges of Nursing
1 Dupont Circle, Suite 530
Washington, DC 20036

American Association of Pastoral Counselors
9504-A Lee Highway
Fairfax, VA 22301

American Association of State Social Work Boards
400 South Ridge Parkway, Suite B
Culpeper, VA 22701

American College Personnel Association
One Dupont Circle, Suite 300
Washington, DC 20036-1110

American Correctional Association
8025 Laurel Lakes Court
Laurel, MD 20707-5075

American Counseling Association
5999 Stevenson Avenue
Alexandria, VA 22304

American Dance Therapy Association
2000 Century Plaza, Suite 106
Columbia, MD 21044

American Health Care Association
1201 L Street, NW
Washington, DC 20005

American Medical Association
515 State Street
Chicago, IL 60610

American Mental Health Counselors Association
AMHCA Central
P. O. Drawer 22370
Alexandria, VA 22304

American Nurses' Association
600 Maryland Avenue, SW, Suite 100W
Washington, DC 20024-2571

American Occupational Therapy Association
P. O. Box 1725
1383 Piccard Drive
Rockville, MD 20849-1725

American Occupational Therapy Certification Board
4 Research Place, Suite 160
Rockville, MD 20850-3226

American Physical Therapy Association
1111 N. Fairfax Street
Alexandria, VA 22314

American Psychological Association
750 1st Street, NE
Washington, DC 20002-4242

American Rehabilitation Counseling Association
5999 Stevenson Avenue
Alexandria, VA 22304

American School Counselor Association
5999 Stevenson Avenue
Alexandria, VA 22304

American Society for Group Psychotherapy and Psychodrama
6728 Old McLean Village Drive
McLean, VA 22101

American Speech-Language-Hearing Association
10801 Rockville Pike
Rockville, MD 20852

American Therapeutic Recreation Association
P. O. Box 15215
Hattiesburg, MS 39404-5215

Association for Adult Development and Aging
5999 Stevenson Avenue
Alexandria, VA 22304

Association for Counselor Education and Supervision
5999 Stevenson Avenue
Alexandria, VA 22304

Association for Counselors and Educators in Government
5999 Stevenson Avenue
Alexandria, VA 22304

Association for Multicultural Counseling and Development
5999 Stevenson Avenue
Alexandria, VA 22304

Association of College and University Housing Officers-International
101 Curl Drive, Suite 140
Columbus, OH 43210

Association of Fraternity Advisors
3901 W. 86th Street, Suite 390
Indianapolis, IN 46208

Association of State and Provincial Psychology Boards
P. O. Box 4389
Montgomery, AL 36103

Certification Board for Music Therapists, Inc.
6336 N. Oracle Road, Suite 326
Tucson, AZ 85704-5457

Cooperative Education Association
11710 Beltsville Drive, Suite 520
Beltsville, MD 20705

Council for Accreditation of Counseling and Related Educational Programs
5999 Stevenson Avenue
Alexandria, VA 22304

Council for the National Register of Health Service Providers in Psychology
1120 G. Street, NW, Suite 330
Washington, DC 20005

Council on Social Work Education
1600 Duke Street, Suite 300
Alexandria, VA 22314

Federal Probation and Pretrial Officers Association
c/o U. S. Pretrial Services Agency
225 Cadman Plaza East
Brooklyn, NY 11201

International Association of Addictions and Offender Counselors
5999 Stevenson Avenue
Alexandria, VA 22304

International Association of Counseling Services
101 S. Whitting, Suite 211
Alexandria, VA 22304

International Association of Marriage and Family Counseling
5999 Stevenson Avenue
Alexandria, VA 22304

National Association for Campus Activities
13 Harbison Way
Columbia, SC 29212

National Association for Drama Therapy
44 Taylor Place
Branford, CT 06405

National Association for Music Therapy
8455 Colesville Road, Suite 930
Silver Spring, MD 20910

National Association for Poetry Therapy
Box 551
Port Washington, NY 11050

National Association for Practical Nurse Education and Service, Inc.
1400 Spring Street, Suite 310
Silver Spring, MD 20910

National Association for Women in Education
1325 18th Street, NW, #210
Washington, DC 20036-6511

National Association of Social Workers
750 1st Street, NE, Suite 700
Washington, DC 20002

National Association of Student Employment Administrators
P. O. Box 1428
Princeton, NJ 08542

National Association of Student Personnel Administrators
1875 Connecticut Avenue., NW, Suite 418
Washington, DC 20009

National Board for Certified Counselors
3 Terrace Way, Suite D
Greensboro, NC 27403

National Career Development Association
5999 Stevenson Avenue
Alexandria, VA 22304

National Clearing House for Commuter Programs
University of Maryland
1195 Adel H. Stamp Student Union
College Park, MD 20742

National Council for Therapeutic Recreation Certification
49 S. Main Street, Suite 001
Spring Valley, NY 10977

National Employment Counseling Association
5999 Stevenson Avenue
Alexandria, VA 22304

National Federation of Licensed Practical Nurses, Inc.
P. O. Box 18088
Raleigh, NC 27619

National Intramural & Recreation Sports Association
850 S. W. 15th Street
Corvallis, OR 97333

National League for Nursing
350 Hudson Street
New York, NY 10014

National Organization for Human Services Education
Box 6257
Fitchburg State College
Fitchburg, NJ 01420

National Orientation Directors Association
University of Tennesee, Knoxville
412 Student Services
Knoxville, TN 37996

National Parks and Recreation Association
Division of Professional Services
2775 S. Quincy Street, Suite 300
Arlington, VA 22206-2204

National Rehabilitation Counseling Association
8807 Sudley Road, Suite 102
Manassas, VA 22110-4719

National Society for Experiential Education
3509 Haworth Drive, Suite 207
Raleigh, NC 27609-7229

National Therapeutic Recreation Society
2775 S. Quincy Street, Suite 300
Arlington, VA 22206-2204

MATRIX OF OCCUPATIONAL TITLES AND WORK SETTINGS

JOB TITLE/ OCCUPATION	License (L) Certification (C) MAY BE Required	WORK SETTING							
		School Counseling	Post-Secondary Institutions	Business & Industry	Private Practice	Public & Private Agencies	Federal & State Agencies	Health Care Facilities	Residential Treatment Centers
Academic Advisor			●						
Administrator		●	●	●	○	●	○	●	○
Admissions Counselor			●						
Black Student Advisor		○	●						
Business Manager			●	○	○	○	○	○	○
Career Consultant	C	○	●	○	○				
Career Counselor			●	●	●	○	○	○	○
Case Manager						○	○	○	●
Case Worker						○	○	○	○
Chancellor			●						
Clinical Mental Health Counselor	C		○	○	●	●	○	○	○
Coach			●						
Consultant			●	○	●	○	○	●	○
Consulting Psychologist	L		○	○	○	○	○	○	○
Coordinator of Freshman Experience			●						
Coordinator of Special Services			●						
Correction Counselor/ Psychologist	L/C						●		
Counselor	C	●	●	●	●	●	●	●	●
Dance Therapist	C							●	○

JOB TITLE/ OCCUPATION	License (L) Certification (C) MAY BE Required	School Counseling	Post-Secondary Institutions	Business & Industry	Private Practice	Public & Private Agencies	Federal & State Agencies	Health Care Facilities	Residential Treatment Centers
WORK SETTING									
Dean of Admissions			●						
Dean of Freshmen			●						
Dean of Student Affairs			●						
Director of Academic Advising			●						
Director of Athletics			●						
Director of Campus Activities			●						
Director of Career Planning			●						
Direcror of Commuter Programs			●						
Director of Couseling	L/C	●	●		○	○	○	○	○
Director of Greek Life			●						
Director of Housing/ Residence Life			●						
Director of Judicial Programs			●						
Director of Learning Skills Center			●						
Director of Minority Program			●						
Director of Orientation			●						
Director of Residence Life			●						
Director of Student Union			●						
EAP Professional		○	○	●	○	○	○	○	○
Employment Counselor					○		●	○	○
Employment Interviewer				●					
Employment Recruiter				●					

JOB TITLE/ OCCUPATION	License (L) Certification (C) MAY BE Required	School Counseling	Post-Secondary Institutions	Business & Industry	Private Practice	Public & Private Agencies	Federal & State Agencies	Health Care Facilities	Residential Treatment Centers
				WORK SETTING					
Family Counselor	C	○		●	○	○	○	○	○
Gerontological Counselor	C			●	○	○	○	○	○
Head Resident/Hall Director			●						
Health Psychologist	L		○	○	○	○	○	●	○
Human Resources Director			●	●		○	○	○	○
Hypnotherapist					○			○	
International Student Advisor			●						
Learning Skills Specialist			●		○		○	○	○
Licensed Professional Counselor	L	●	○	○	●	●	○	○	○
Marriage and Family Counselor	L/C	○		○		○	○	○	○
Mediation Counselor					●				
Mental Health Counselor	L/C			○	●	●	○	○	●
Military Counselor							●		
Music Therapist	C				○		○	●	○
Neuropsychologist	L				○	○	○	●	●
Nurse	L	●	○	○	○	●	○	●	●
Occupational Therapist	L					○	○	●	●
Parole Officer							●		
Personnel Manager		○	○	●		○	○	○	○
Physical Therapist	L				○	○	○	●	●
Physician	L	○	●	○	○	○	○	●	●
President			●	○					
Probation Officer							●		
Professional Counselor	L/C	●	○	○	●	●	○	○	○
Psychiatric Aide	C					●	○	●	●
Psychiatrist	L	●	●	○	○	●	○	●	○
Psychologist (Clinical, Counseling)	L	●	●	○	●	●	●	●	●

147

JOB TITLE/ OCCUPATION	License (L) Certification (C) MAY BE Required	School Counseling	Post-Secondary Institutions	Business & Industry	Private Practice	Public & Private Agencies	Federal & State Agencies	Health Care Facilities	Residential Treatment Centers
WORK SETTING									
Psychology Technician					O	O	O	●	O
Psychometrist			●		O	O	O	O	O
Psychotherapist					●	O	O	O	O
Recreation Therapist/Aide	L/C				O	O	O	●	●
Registrar			●						
Rehabilitation Counselor	C				●	O	●	●	●
Retirement Counselor				O	O	O	O	O	O
School Counselor	C	●							
School Psychologist	L/C	●							
Social Worker (Clinical, School)	L	●	●		O	●	O	O	●
Student Employment Coordinator	C		●						
Substance Abuse Counselor	C	O	●	O	O	O	O	O	O
Teacher		●	O		●				
Therapist					●	O	●	O	O
Training Director			●			O	O	O	
University Vice President			●						
Vocational Rehabilitation Counselor	C				O	O	●	O	O
Wellness Counselor			O	O	O			O	O
Youth Counselor							●	O	O

●   Indicates occupations that are discussed in that chapter.

O   Indicates occupations that exist in that work setting, but are not discussed in that chapter.

148

Index

Organizational Consultant 62
Outplacement Counselor 3, 58
Panhellenic or Intrafraternity Council Advisor 49
Parole Officer 73
Personnel Representative 51
Physical Therapist 3, 95, 106
Physician 35, 44, 95, 102
Physician's Assistant 44
Police Officer 29
Principal 23
Private Practitioner 3, 65-72
Probation Officer or Worker 82
Programming Coordinator 49
Psychiatrist 10, 44, 95
Psychiatric Technician 73
Psychological Services Associate 73
Psychologist 3, 10, 32, 95, 99
Psychology Technicians 116
Psychiatric Aide 116
Psychiatric Nursing Assistant 116
Psychiatric Technician 116
Psychometrist 42
Recreation Aide 3, 49
Recreation Therapist 109, 117
Registrar 39
Rehabilitation Counselor 3, 43, 102
Residence Hall Complex Coordinator 2
Resident Assistants 47
School Counselor 2, 6, 20-30
School Principal 28
School Psychologist 28-29
School Social Workers 28-29
Senior Student Affairs Officer 38
Social Services Worker 22
Social Worker 3, 10, 32, 73, 95, 97-99, 118
Speech-Language Therapist 3
Staff Counselor 42
Staff Psychologist 42
Student Activities Program Coordinator 2
Student Activity Advisor 49
Student Affairs Professionals 31